Immigration and Strategic Public Health Communication

‖‖‖‖‖‖‖‖‖‖‖‖‖‖‖‖‖‖‖‖
I0129068

This book engages a key question facing governments and similar institutions in countries of immigration or emigration: how should these governments and institutions communicate with immigrants so that they will listen to and act on their messages?

Drawing on original research with Mexican emigrants in New York and the Mexican government's Seguro Popular health care program, the authors examine the ways in which governments integrate migrants into diasporic political, medical, educational, and other systems, and how migrant-sending countries communicate with their emigrants abroad. In analyzing how these efforts fail or succeed, this book presents strategies and policy recommendations that many governments and institutions can use to engage their citizens or clients ethically and effectively.

Offering a valuable approach to the study of race, migration, and public policy, this book will be of key importance to researchers and graduate students in public health, sociology, marketing and business, political science, Latinx studies, and international communication.

Robert Courtney Smith is a Professor in the Marxe School of Public and International Affairs at Baruch College, and the Sociology Department of The Graduate Center, City University of New York (CUNY). He wrote *Mexican New York: Transnational Worlds of New Immigrants* (2006), which won the 2008 Distinguished Book Award from the American Sociological Association and five other prizes. He was a Guggenheim Fellow and has been funded by the National Science Foundation, W.T. Grant foundation, Russell Sage Foundation, Social Science Research Council, and others. He serves as Board Chair of Masa (masany.org).

Don J. Waisanen is an Associate Professor in the Marxe School of Public and International Affairs at Baruch College, CUNY, where he teaches courses and workshops in public communication—including executive speech training, communication strategy, and seminars on leadership, storytelling, and improvisation. All his research projects seek to understand how communication works to promote or hinder the force of citizens' voices, including his recent book, *Political Conversion: Personal Transformation as Strategic Public Communication*. He is the founder of Communication Upward (commupward.com), an adjunct lecturer at Columbia University and New York University, and received a PhD in Communication from the University of Southern California's Annenberg School.

Guillermo Yrizar Barbosa is a PhD candidate in sociology at The Graduate Center, and data manager at Baruch College, CUNY. He has been (2018–2019) a research associate and coordinator for the Legislation and Migration Policy Observatory at El Colegio de la Frontera Norte in Tijuana, and a Visiting Research Fellow (2017–2018) at the Center for US-Mexico Studies, University of California, San Diego, School of Global Policy and Strategy. He was a fellow at the CUNY Institute for Demographic Research (2014–2017).

Routledge Research in Health Communication

Immigration and Strategic Public Health Communication

Lessons from the Transnational Seguro Popular Project

Robert Courtney Smith,
Don J. Waisanen, and
Guillermo Yrizar Barbosa

Routledge
Taylor & Francis Group

LONDON AND NEW YORK

First published 2020 by Routledge

2 Park Square, Milton Park, Abingdon, Oxon OX14 4RN
605 Third Avenue, New York, NY 10017

Routledge is an imprint of the Taylor & Francis Group, an informa business

First issued in paperback 2021

Publisher's Note

The publisher has gone to great lengths to ensure the quality of this reprint but points out that some imperfections in the original copies may be apparent.

Library of Congress Cataloging-in-Publication Data
A catalog record for this title has been requested

ISBN: 978-0-367-27765-9 (hbk)
ISBN: 978-1-03-217783-0 (pbk)
DOI: 10.4324/9780367334819

Typeset in Times New Roman
by codeMantra

Contents

Figures

Tables

Acknowledgments

The Principal Investigator, Robert Smith, would like to thank the original Seguro Popular research team, including Eduardo Peñaloza (instrumental in establishing and conducting the first project); Julio César García Torres (who created videos for social media public service promotions); Wei Ting Lu (who ran all the statistics for Chapter 2); Liliana Durán; Tommy Wu; Angelo Cabrera; Jasniya Sánchez; Calixto Domingo; Jesús Meza; and others who helped with the project, including Karen Chavez, Teresita Prieto, Sharenny Díaz, Sara Guerrero Rippberger, Ismelda Rosario, and Peter Cipriano. Special thanks go to our partners at the Mexican Consulate in New York: Ambassador Carlos Sada and consular staff Josana Tonda Salcedo, Dante Gómez, Isai Hernández, and Nilbia Coyote. At Seguro Popular and the Centro de Investigación y Docencia Económicas (CIDE), we are especially grateful to José Francisco Caballero, Claudia Jazmín Segovia Rojo, Karin González, and María Dolores Ramírez Serrano, who offered excellent feedback on drafts of the reports and during their periodic visits. We would also like to express our gratitude to all participants and community leaders who shared their concerns, ideas, and opinions with us, including Daniel Olvera Posada, Bernardo Garza, and transnational families from Tlaxcala in Queens. This book is a joint project, with varying levels of authorial work. It stems from the work done on SegPop1 ("How much immigrants know about Seguro Popular," which underpins Chapter 2) and SegPop2 ("How to talk to immigrants…," which underpins the rest of the book). Robert Smith drafted the entire first report, with assistance from the SegPop team (including Guillermo Yrizar), and drafted most of the second report, along with Don Waisanen, on social marketing and assistance from the SegPop team. The reports were redrafted into this book by iterative revisions by Robert Smith, Don Waisanen, and Guillermo Yrizar, its main academic authors.

We extend special thanks and recognition to Manuel Castro, the Executive Director of New Immigrant Community Empowerment (NICE), and Aracelis Lucero, Executive Director of Masa. It was Manuel Castro's initial insight to propose using a social marketing approach to study and structure institution/government-immigrant communication, and he did excellent work in obtaining and analyzing the focus-group and interview data. Aracelis Lucero organized much of the teamwork for both projects. Castro and Lucero worked with the three academic authors to design and administer the focus groups and interviews for Chapter 3. Castro is now using these approaches in their management of key nonprofit organizations working with immigrants and their families in New York (NICE and Masa, respectively).

1 Seguro Popular, Diasporic Bureaucracies, and Social Marketing

This book started with curious, counterintuitive questions. Officials from the Seguro Popular (SP) government health care office visited Robert Smith (Principal Investigator on this project) at the City University of New York and asked if Mexican immigrants in NY would use this public health policy in Mexico. Do migrants even know about the program? Do New York–residing migrants' families in Mexico use SP now? And could we approach Mexican immigrants in NY to promote use of this program by their families in Mexico? These officials suspected that migrant families weren't using SP as much as they could and that returning migrants weren't using it at all.

At first glance, these questions make little sense. Why market a health policy or program based in Mexico to migrants in the US? Why not just market directly to their families in Mexico? Yet the questions make perfect sense in the context of decades of Mexican migration to the US and New York. Some evidence indicates that migrants returning to Mexico have worse health and greater health care needs (Arenas et al., 2015). Moreover, these questions align with the Mexican government's increasing efforts to develop what Smith (2008) calls *diasporic bureaucracies* to cultivate links with its migrants abroad and promote the positive integration of Mexicans into the US, especially in the last 25 years. That Mexican government officials working in a program offering health services only in Mexico would promote its use by New York–residing migrants and their Mexico-residing families reflects how transnationalized some dimensions of Mexican migrant life have become and how the Mexican government has sought to engage its diaspora on key issues in migrant life, including health. Indeed, SP officials approached us with a pamphlet designed for outreach to immigrants in NY, the cover page which is reproduced below (Figure 1.1). The initial research on how much Mexican immigrants in NY knew about SP and how much they or their families used it,

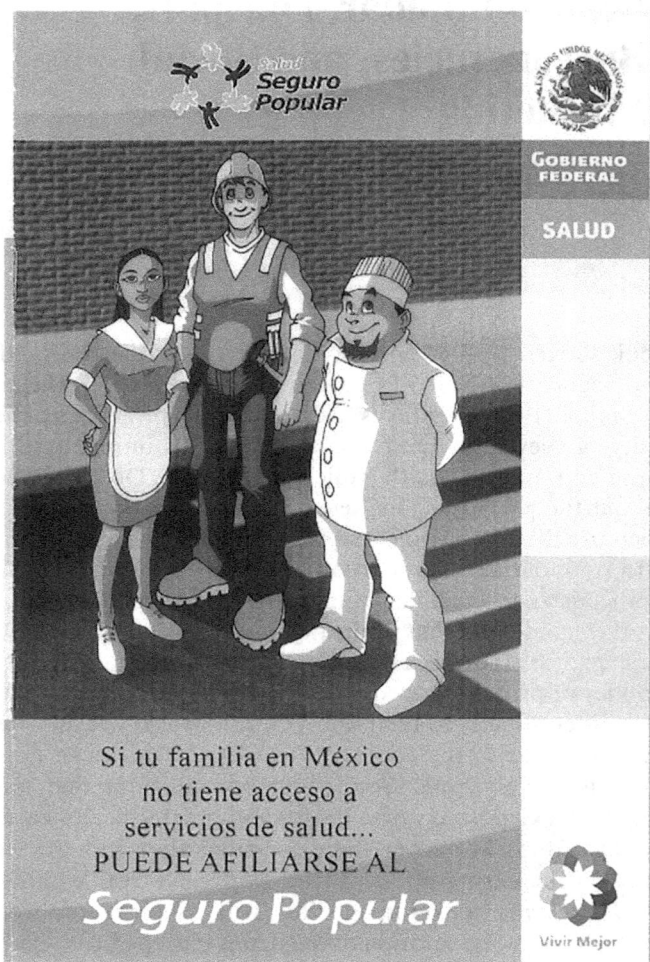

Figure 1.1 Cover of a Pamphlet or Comic Book in Spanish, Designed by the Mexican Government to Promote SP among Mexicans in the United States, Stating, "If Your Family in Mexico Does Not Have Access to Health Services ... It Can Enroll in Seguro Popular."

presented in Chapter 2, led to the second project, constituting the main analytical work of this book. We seek to understand how Mexico's efforts to reach out to its diaspora were understood or misunderstood by immigrants, and how it might do better.

While the empirical grounding for this book is Mexico's attempts to promote the use of SP among migrants and their families, this opens a larger theoretical and policy conversation about how governments and institutions should communicate with immigrants so that they will actually listen, including in their own messaging and via different platforms such as social media. Given the growth in the immigrant population in the US and other traditional receiving countries in recent decades, it's imperative for governments and institutions to know how to communicate with immigrants and their children to promote positive integration into their new societies.

The SP project underlines a fundamental contradiction between the transnational lives of many migrants and their families, and the local, state, and national governmental entities that deliver public services. The nation-state and its subdivisions are organized for service delivery by territory but also by formal membership category. Those in the territory with full membership are entitled to services such as access to the labor market or health care, while those lacking such membership are not. We discuss this issue more at length in Chapter 4, but we highlight a crisis that can also be seen as an opportunity for the Mexican state: returned and vulnerable migrants in general and, more specifically, *Los Otros Dreamers* ("The Other Dreamers"), Mexicans who get deported back to Mexico from the US, after living there for years (Anderson & Solis, 2014; see also Landa, 2014). Many left Mexico as babies and were raised in the US, speak English fluently, don't know Mexico, and may have their own US-born, US-citizen children. They're essentially being deported to a foreign country. Moreover, most parents who are deported have "mixed status" families. The result is that about a half-million Mexicans who grew up in the US but were deported now live in Mexico, and another half-million US-citizen children are enrolled in Mexican schools, after coming back with their families (Anderson, 2015; Anderson & Solis, 2014; Escobar Latapí, Lowell, & Martin, 2013; Zuñiga, 2015; Zuñiga & Hamann, 2008). These *retornados* ("returnees") are low-hanging fruit for enrollment in health policies such as SP, which has already been working to enroll them. These steps are to be applauded, and they should be expanded: they offer a welcoming hand by the Mexican government to its *retornado* population. We return to this issue in Chapter 4.

This book develops insights from the SP research project in New York. It does three kinds of analytical work. First, it describes the SP project in NY, presenting new research on what immigrants knew about this health policy and what factors affected immigrants' or their families' knowledge or use of it. It offers a demographic and social profile of Mexicans in NY as critical for Mexico to use in approaching its diaspora. It also adds to the growing literature on Mexican immigrants in new destination cities, including NY, America's archetypal city of immigrants (Foner, 2013), which epitomizes a demographic transition to diversity (Alba & Yrizar Barbosa, 2016).

Second, the book analyzes the SP project as a public service promotion by a diasporic bureaucracy—an institution created by a home country to work with its immigrants abroad—specifically, to learn how to engage with immigrants and promote programs improving the well-being of immigrant families in Mexico and the US. We recognize that most of our recommendations haven't been carried out, but we emphasize the fact that Mexico and other sending states have created and developed diasporic bureaucracies to attend to relations with immigrants abroad, with a long-term interest in health. Commissioning the SP project demonstrates Mexico's interest in learning how to develop such links. In this vein, the book proposes a set of actions that could further deepen links between Mexico and its citizens abroad via diasporic bureaucracies, including through social media and other methods. Because the central object of analysis isn't SP as a health policy or program in itself, but rather Mexico's interest in promoting its use among immigrants in NY, we only briefly assess that program's political and public health meaning. We spend more time on how Mexico's current and previous approaches to its diaspora have been understood, and how Mexico and similar countries might do this communicative work better.[1]

Third, our research offers insights into how governments and institutions should communicate with immigrants and their families, including what language and methods to use in their approaches. A key finding is that the words and framing will be understood by immigrants within the context of the larger immigrant-institutional relationship. Two examples are illustrative.

Immigrants in our research rejected the form of address that the Mexican government has been using for two decades in its Programa Paisano (a program designed, among other things, to thwart the extortion of returning migrants by Mexican customs officials), Programa 3 × 1 (a community development matching-fund program with collective remittances), Grupos Beta (the humanitarian corps/agency to assist and protect migrants in Mexico), and other federal programs. The term *migrante* ("migrant") was resented by immigrants in our study because, for them, it emphasized the difference in power between immigrants who were forced to come to the US and consular personnel, who came voluntarily.

At the same time, our informants rejected SP when it was discussed as a "social right"—the framing that SP uses, based on the Mexican Constitution—but embraced it when it was reframed as "a paid insurance policy," based on exchange (getting a service because you pay for it). Defining this policy as a social right highlighted what many immigrants thought was the Mexican government's broken social contract that had forced them to leave their country to begin with, whereas the payment-for-service framing made them contractually equal parties. This implies that to assess the communication and social marketing strategies that governments, institutions, and organizations should take to persuade immigrants to take action (e.g., enrolling in health care programs), they should do specific research to understand how their audience will interpret language choices.

This book contributes to our understanding of how Mexican and US (and other) institutions and governments can and should promote such engagement and action. The book thus makes theoretical contributions to our understanding of how people's identities, relationships, and preferences can best be mobilized in programmatic outreach, including practical, how-to insights for designing such outreach. It should be of special interest in the US, where all levels of government (federal, state, and local) and many institutions (foundations, multilateral agencies, etc.) are seeking to engage immigrants and their children in myriad activities, from promoting pre-K enrollment or school achievement, to developing closer relationships with the police or law enforcement agents, to working more closely with social-services or community-based organizations.

This book presents original findings from the SP project,[2] the result of two research contracts during 2011–2012 between the Centro de Investigación y Docencia Económica (CIDE) in Mexico City, and Baruch College, of the City University of New York (CUNY), completed in consultation with staff at SP and other Mexican government functionaries. While the initial focus of the study was on immigrants' knowledge of and disposition to use this policy, the broader opportunities for this project that we outlined above quickly surfaced. Our conversations with immigrants about their own or their families' use of SP opened questions about how diasporic and other bureaucracies and organizations should talk to immigrants and how they might get them to act in their own interest. This is a significant issue facing governments and private institutions seeking to mobilize immigrants and others toward some goal. The key is that these institutions must talk to immigrants in ways that will get them to listen and to hear *intended* rather than *unintended* messages. This issue plays out in many public-policy issues, from how to get people to wear seat belts, to increasing sign-ups for the Affordable Care Act (Blanding, 2014). We engage these academic and policy conversations throughout this book.

History of SP, Diasporic Bureaucracies, and This Project

Mexico's modern health bureaucracy dates to the 1943 creation of the Secretary of Health and the Instituto Mexicano de Seguro Social (IMSS; Mexican Social Security Institute) and the later creation of the Instituto de Seguridad y Servicios Sociales de los Trabajadores del Estado (ISSSTE; Institute for Social Security and Services for State Workers) in 1959 (Barba Solano, 2010; Córdova Villalobos, 2010; Frenk et al., 2003). The late 1970s saw expansion of a primary-care approach to health care. A key milestone was the 1983 constitutional reform declaring health care a constitutionally guaranteed "social right." This right was enacted more fully in the 2003 Reform of the General Health Law that created the Sistema Nacional de Protección Social en Salud (SNPSS, or simply SPSS).[3] These reforms were broadened by a systematic reorganization of the health care system in the 2001–2006 National Health Plan to create SP in 2004. Seeking the "democratization of health," these reforms sought to enable the national health system to better cover the entire population, particularly those not covered by IMSS or ISSSTE.

SP has taken several measures to attempt to make health care a real social right in Mexico, embodying this constitutional right in institutional practice. First, from its founding during the administration of President Vicente Fox (2000–2006), SP delinked access to health care from employment. If health care access is via one's employment (as in IMSS or ISSSTE), unemployed citizens or those working in the informal economy—over 50% of Mexico's workforce—are effectively denied health care. SP granted program access to anyone who couldn't otherwise access health care, including the unemployed. Second, SP significantly expanded free health services via multiple programs: Seguro Médico para una Nueva Generación (SMNG; Healthcare for a New Generation), to all children born after 2005; the Embarazo Saludable program (Healthy Pregnancy), which offered universal prenatal care; and greater coverage for chronic conditions, e.g., diabetes and catastrophic events, such as recovery from emergency surgery.

These expansions were designed not only to provide a social right to health care but also to fight poverty (they were implemented alongside complementary antipoverty programs like Oportunidades, which gave families cash payments—e.g., for keeping their children in school (Garza, 2015; Knaul et al., 2012; 2015; Laurell, 2014). If mothers had prenatal care and children had regular medical care, they would be healthier and less likely to be poor. If the government could prevent catastrophic health care costs from bankrupting families, fewer children would grow up in poverty. Prior to SP, most poor families without insurance faced an impossible choice: pay for health care or pay for food and necessities. Any special procedure or surgery had to be paid for privately. Many chose not to have medical care. For those who did pay, it crippled family finances for years and diminished educational and other life chances for their children. SP, thus, sought to disrupt this cycle of impoverishment by removing or diminishing the cumulative financial impacts of catastrophic illness. In so doing, it sought to create a social right with legal, financial, and health care benefits that all citizens would enjoy *as citizens*, regardless of ability to pay (Laurell, 2014), and to transform Mexico's public health service into a health-insurance service that would also fight poverty (Lakin, 2010).

SP represents an important attempt by the state to deepen and broaden the health care coverage offered to all Mexicans. The concept of "social rights" is explicit in the Mexican Constitution, which theoretically guarantees a host of rights that the US Constitution does not, including the right to an education, equality for women, and health care. SP represents an attempt by the Mexican state to decrease the sometimes large gap between a key constitutionally guaranteed right and the inability of most Mexicans to exercise it. While not always discussed this way in public debate, SP officials framed it this way to us and saw it as justification for their work.

Research on SP has been both critical and supportive. Some research shows that SP has had positive effects on the health and well-being of Mexicans. King et al. (2007, 2009) analyzed the impacts of SP in Mexico, concluding that it had slashed catastrophic and in-patient and out-patient out-of-pocket expenditures and that citizen satisfaction has generally been high (King, n.d.). Paradoxically, they found that only 66% of those automatically eligible for a parallel complementary program, the Programa de Desarrollo Humano Oportunidades[4] (Human Development Opportunities Program), knew about their automatic eligibility or affiliation (King et al., 2009, p. 1451). Hernández-Torres et al. (2008) also found that catastrophic health spending decreased because of SP. They found less evidence that the program was being used for preventive services, or to reduce larger health-risk factors. SP has improved health access and outcomes for diabetic patients, compared with similar patients not enrolled in the program (Sosa-Rubí,

Galárraga, & López-Ridaura, 2009), and improved health outcomes among patients with hypertension in Mexico (Bleich et al., 2007). By 2013, according to an annual report by the Mexican federal government, 55.6 million people were enrolled in SP, showing real growth, compared with 2004 (5.3 million) and 2010 (43.5 million) (Secretaría de Salud & Seguro Popular, 2014). Knaul et al. (2012) argue that SP has steadily improved its performance by ongoing, evidence-driven evaluations of how its programs have worked, improved overall health, and prevented catastrophic health care expenses from bankrupting families.

Other scholars have been more critical of SP. Laurell (2014) called SP neoliberal health care because it isn't universal, combines public and private institutions, and often requires patients to pay for services, especially for tests or specialists. She also describes it as "segmented and fragmented," compared with plans of other Latin American countries, because labor health care is "mandatory and public," while SP "is voluntary and only the population without labor health care" are eligible (pp. 13–14). SP further required huge financial and bureaucratic investments to become operational. According to Lakin (2010), despite increasing health spending, "expected contributions from states and families have not materialized, leaving the program severely underfinanced and its long-term sustainability threatened" (p. 316). Laurell (2014) argues that large expansions in enrollment in SP are not evidence of significant impact but, rather, of efforts by Mexican states that want the federal funding that follows new enrollees (pp. 117–118). Indeed, some people have been enrolled in the program without their knowledge. SP has left 30 million people uncovered, including, in 2010, some 10.5 million living in "extreme poverty, corresponding to 35.7%" of Mexico's poorest people. Nigenda et al. (2015), using information collected from external evaluations, argue that the implementation of SP confronts major challenges due to "limited institutional capacity" at the federal and state levels, among other political and financial factors, such as "a continuous power struggle between the federal government and states over the implementation of Mexico's health reform" (pp. 224–225). Other researchers have argued that SP has exaggerated its successes and not reformed an unresponsive bureaucracy whose lethargy endangers the public health and negates its intended effects, such as reducing infant mortality or poverty (Díaz, Castañeda Pérez, & Meneses Navarro, 2010, p. 11). Daniela Díaz, of the nonpartisan advocacy group Fundar, argues that the administration of federal funds for SP lacks transparency and that its underperformance at the federal and state levels should be investigated (Alatorre, 2016; see also

Lavielle, 2012). A special journal issue on the Mexican Health System and Reforms focused on these issues, including Garza's (2015) policy recommendations to increase the responsiveness of services provided by SP.

Our goal is to recognize but not resolve these debates about SP and the prevailing health inequalities that Mexico is still facing, despite this policy (Flamand & Moreno Jaimes, 2014), potentially leading to significant changes under the Andrés Manuel López Obrador administration. Research shows that SP *has* improved access to health care and health outcomes for many Mexicans, especially those who weren't covered under previous systems, for routine (e.g., birth of a child) as well as catastrophic events (some types of cancer), but that it has fallen far short of its goal of universal health care and has become a target of criticism over funding. Setting this debate aside for now, we turn to the questions leading to this study of immigrants and SP in New York.

SP raises interesting questions for Mexico regarding the goal of reaching universal health care, its nationals living abroad (11.7 million in 2014), and the development of dissemination campaigns in the US (where 98% of Mexicans abroad reside): how much would immigrants know or not know about SP? How much would they use its services? And how would Mexico promote the program's use among those in the "migration belt" of Mexico or across the different migration sending regions? Research on the relationship between migration and health comes to varying conclusions, but findings that returning migrants tend to be in worse health would support the logic of marketing SP to migrants abroad (Arenas et al., 2015; see also Wilson, Stimpson, & Pagan, 2014; Escobar Latapí et al., 2013; Oristian et al., 2009; Salgado et al., 2012).

Several studies link health status with different types of return migrants from Mexico. Using the Mexican Family Life Survey, Arenas et al. (2015) found higher probabilities of return migration for Mexican migrants in poor health and lower probabilities of return for those with improving health. Wilson et al. (2014) state that legal immigrants "did not have a significantly higher risk of having a self-reported diagnosis of hypertension, diabetes, heart or lung problems, or poor mental health compared to nonmigrants," but nevertheless, "the hazard ratio for unauthorized deported immigrants" was higher for diabetes and poor mental health, compared with nonmigrants (p. 1). A case study in a community of high emigration in central western Mexico showed that "returned migrants reported higher rates of asthma, high blood pressure, heart problems, and muscle problems than do migrants who stay in the US, and they are only slightly less likely to report obesity or high cholesterol." However, returning migrants "are less likely than US-based migrants to report an infirmity, indicating that they are relatively healthy" (Oristian et al., 2009, pp. 221–225). A binational policy-oriented research team found that migrants have bad health conditions in both countries—especially, returned migrants, who are less healthy than older individuals who didn't migrate out of Mexico and less healthy than those who stayed in the US (Border Health Commission, 2011; Salgado et al., 2012). This evidence shows that officials of programs and policies like SP have been right to try to build connections with and improve the health outcomes of Mexicans with international migration experience.

The SP officials' hunch that migrants and their families weren't using this health policy as much as they might is at least partly supported by our analysis of the overlap between migration and per-capita spending on SP, presented in Figure 1.2 below. This map shows that six states (Aguascalientes, Colima, Durango, Hidalgo, Nayarit, and Zacatecas) with high or very high rates of migratory intensity have lower levels of per-capita spending on SP ($467–$720; Mexican pesos), while four (Guerrero, Oaxaca, Morelos, and San Luis Potosí) with high levels

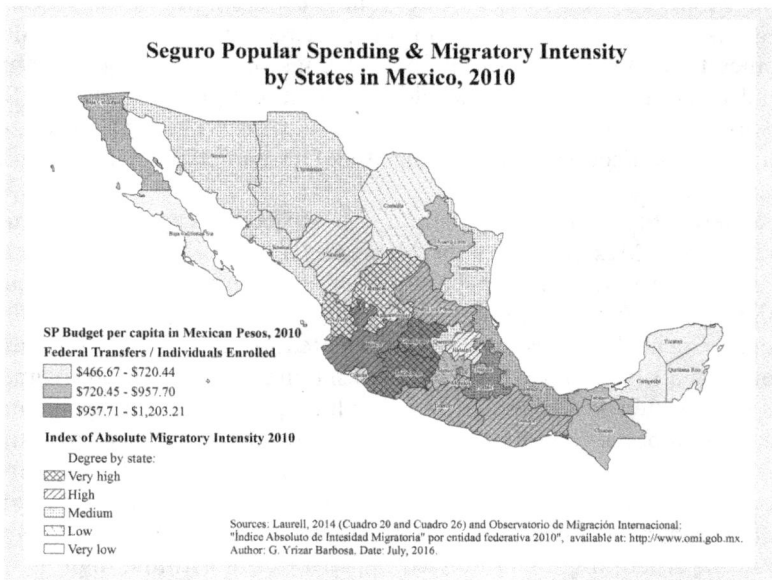

Seguro Popular Spending & Migratory Intensity by States in Mexico, 2010

SP Budget per capita in Mexican Pesos, 2010
Federal Transfers / Individuals Enrolled
- $466.67 - $720.44
- $720.45 - $957.70
- $957.71 - $1,203.21

Index of Absolute Migratory Intensity 2010
Degree by state:
- Very high
- High
- Medium
- Low
- Very low

Sources: Laurell, 2014 (Cuadro 20 and Cuadro 26) and Observatorio de Migración Internacional: "Índice Absoluto de Intesidad Migratoria" por entidad federativa 2010", available at: http://www.omi.gob.mx. Author: G. Yrizar Barbosa. Date: July, 2016.

Figure 1.2 SP Spending and Migratory Intensity by States in Mexico, 2010.

of migratory intensity have medium levels of spending ($721–$958). Only three (Guanajuato, Jalisco, and Michoacán) with very high or high levels of migratory intensity have high levels of per-capita spending (above $958: only five states out of the 32). While not conclusive, this quick analysis suggests an inverse relationship between migratory intensity and per-capita spending on SP—states with more migrants tend to spend less on SP.

Diasporic Bureaucracies and the SP Project

Mexico's interest in addressing the needs of its nationals abroad isn't unique in the history of state–diaspora relationships. During the last great wave of migration to the US, sending states and their diasporas were in close contact and sought to cultivate and maintain relations with their emigrants abroad and protect them in their adopted lands. Such efforts continue today, even among countries that are mainly immigrant receiving but that also have significant numbers of migrants abroad. Such state–diasporic relationships are driven by a host of issues central to any national community, including remittances (which help the sending state financially), influence on home-country policies toward the sending country (a foreign-policy issue for the sending state), and voting from abroad (enabling immigrants or expatriates living outside their country of birth or citizenship to vote in that country's elections, recognizing them as members of the national community; Bauböck, 2007; Bauböck & Faist, 2010; Collyer, 2013; Faist, 1995; Fitzgerald, 2009; Gonzáles Gutiérrez, 2006; Green & Waldinger, 2016; Lafleur, 2011; Schmitter, 1985; Waldinger, 2015; Yrizar Barbosa, 2008, 2009. Countries of destination have, of course, crafted policies to decide which immigrants to let in, for how long, and under what conditions (Fitzgerald & Cook-Martin, 2014; Zolberg, 2006).

Diasporic policies linked to Italian migration in the late 1880s–early/mid-1900s migration and Mexican migration today can usefully be compared. In the late 1880s–early 1990s, Italy's General Commission on Emigration (later replaced by the General Bureau of Italians Abroad) was in charge of protecting Italians' rights but also of creating institutions to maintain and strengthen their links with their homeland (Cordasco, 1980; Foerster, 1919; Smith, 2003a, 2003b, 2006, 2008). Moreover, after World War II, Italy worked with receiving states that didn't want Italian workers to permanently settle (e.g., in France or Germany) to create what Schmitter Heisler (1984) called "exclaves," or institutionalized communities oriented more toward their country of origin than their country of settlement. Other Italian institutions, such as the Scalabrinian missionaries, were dedicated to ministering to Italian immigrants abroad, in Europe and the Americas, and to cultivating Italian nationalism and identity among them. Some scholars have noted that many Italian immigrants identified more with their villages or regions than with Italy as a whole when they left their homeland, but came to identify as Italian when treated as such in their new homes and by Italian emissaries like the Scalabrinians or staff from diasporic bureaucracies (Choate, 2009; Gabaccia, 2000; Smith, 2003a, 2003b, 2008). Following the steps of Italians in the US, other sending states have created state–diaspora programs to maintain these relationships, including Spain, Portugal, India, Morocco, Philippines, Mexico, and Ecuador (Asis & Baggio, 2008; Brand, 2006; Délano, 2011; Herrera, Moncayo, & Escobar, 2012; Iskander, 2010; Sharma, 2006; Solé, 1995).

Further comparing the Mexican and Italian cases highlights a key difference between many contemporary and previous migrant-sending state–diaspora relations. Whereas most Italian immigrants in the late 1800s–early 1900s came with, or quickly achieved, legal resident status, or easily became US citizens and hence could reunify their families if they wished, contemporary Mexican and other immigrants often remain in long-term undocumented status, making family reunification more difficult and creating even more disadvantaged circumstances for Mexican immigrants and their children. These circumstances have tilted the work that the Mexican state (and others with large undocumented populations) conducts with its diaspora to help with these issues. For example, a key problem for long-term undocumented immigrants is lack of necessary secure identification to interact with institutions in the US or other destination countries. In NY, the New York Immigration Coalition (NYIC) successfully lobbied NY's government to recognize, and encouraged the Mexican Consulate to develop, the Matrícula Consular, a secure ID issued by the consulate to identify the immigrant. This resolved vital everyday issues, such as undocumented immigrant parents who couldn't enter their US-citizen children's schools to visit teachers because the parents lacked the requisite ID to enter NYC public schools and other public buildings, which became increasingly necessary after 9/11. The Mexican government developed a set of binational policies to help these immigrant and binational families—e.g., creating Plazas Communitarias, enabling immigrants to continue their precollege educations online, in the US or in Mexico, or through health and labor initiatives in collaboration with local or state-level US authorities and organizational partners (Bada & Gleeson, 2015; Carrasco-Garrido et al., 2009; Marietta, 2006; Martínez-Wenzl, 2013; Sánchez-Siller & Gabarrot-Arenas, 2015; Schmid, 2017; Shtarkshall, Baynesan, & Feldman, 2009; Vázquez et al., 2011;

Weissman et al., 2018). Mexico isn't alone in promoting cross-border health care, as studies on Turks in Denmark, Ethiopians in Israel, and West Africans in the US show (Asamani-Asante, 2014; Nielsen et al., 2012; Shtarkshall et al., 2009).

The range of intents and actions in such diasporic bureaucracies has been broad. Sending states usually create diasporic bureaucracies when their position in the geostrategic system changes, their immigrants begin making autonomous demands, and the place of immigrants in the national community becomes a political issue. Creating a diasporic program usually helps political elites resolve some domestic political issue (Délano, 2011, 2018; Gambetta, 2012; Lafleur, 2011, 2012; Shibata, 2015; Smith, 2003a, 2003b, 2008; Yrizar Barbosa, 2008, 2009; Yrizar Barbosa & Alarcón, 2010).[5] The type of diasporic bureaucracy created varies by each regime, its hold on power, and the country's place in the global system. During the 1960s–1970s, Turkey's programs for its diaspora in Germany were believed by many to function as surveillance for dissidents, as a means of keeping an eye on their organizing efforts abroad (Miller, 1981). Many contemporary immigrants similarly don't work closely with their consulates in the US, feeling they're extensions of governments seeking to control dissent more than offer concrete help (Graham, 2001; Guarnizo, 1998).

Mexico has become a poster child over the last 20 years among immigrant-sending states seeking to develop programs to cultivate ties with their own diasporas. At a conference in Mexico City in the early 2000s, representatives of most major sending states presented summaries of their own programs but also expressed avid interest in how Mexico had developed relationships with its diaspora, especially the concrete steps it was taking and who/what was funding its work. The first author recalls a high-ranking representative of Haiti's diasporic bureaucracy, who presided over its older but less well-developed program, as eager to talk with his Mexican counterparts and impressed at the range of activities they had been able to organize. Other Latin American sending countries similarly looked to Mexico for guidance. These meetings resulted in a book published by Mexico's Secretary of Foreign Affairs in 2006, *State–Diaspora Relations: Approaches from Four Continents*, edited by Carlos González Gutiérrez, a principal architect of Mexico's diasporic strategy, and now Mexico's consul general in Sacramento, California (González Gutiérrez, 1999, 2006; see also Besserer, 2004; Délano, 2011, 2018; Fox & Bada, 2008; Fox & Rivera-Salgado, 2004; Glick-Schiller, Basch, & Szanton-Blanc, 1995; Goldring, 1998; Irazuzta & Yrizar, 2006; Levitt, 2001; Moctezuma, 2015; Pries, 2017; Smith, 1998, 2003a, 2003b, 2006, 2008).

Mexico's stated goals in this work have been to promote immigrant integration into the US and deepen Mexico's relationships with these immigrants (Délano, 2018; González Gutiérrez, 1999; Smith, 2006, 2008). The work engages three distinct kinds of relationships. First, it means promoting contact between Mexicans in the US and the US-based institutions serving those communities—hospitals, schools, universities, etc.—to foster better integration into the US. Second, it implies deepening collaborative relationships between migrants and their communities of origin. This includes programs supporting the work of hometown associations (HTAs) (Escala Rabadán, 2016). The third kind of program recognizes the complexity of transnational life and seeks to address needs stemming from being "between" the two countries. For example, in the Programa 3 × 1, immigrants in the US and their Mexico-residing relatives could choose (in consultation with local authorities) public projects to support. Each dollar the immigrants sent would be matched by a dollar from the local or state government and the federal government. Such projects sometimes exposed the interests of immigrants and nonmigrants. Nonmigrants would ask: why build a sports field (that immigrants could play on when they returned) when we need a new school or clinic more? (Goldring, 1998; Moctezuma, 2015; Smith, 2003). The larger point is that the 3 × 1 structure adopted by the federal government recognized that immigrants were settled in the US but still had interests and legitimate claims on Mexico's public resources because they were contributing, ongoing members of their communities of origin.

These federal programs followed a path forged by state-level governments. Recognizing the contributions of HTAs, immigrants in Los Angeles, Chicago, Texas, and other areas formed state-level federations in the 1980s–1990s to advocate for themselves vis-à-vis their state governments and governors, who were often quicker to respond than the federal government. The most famous federation is the Zacatecanos, formed in the mid-1980s, whose close collaboration with the governor and state government of Zacatecas has been well documented (Goldring, 1998; Moctezuma, 2015; Smith, 2003). These collaborations have included sponsoring the construction of public works in Mexico, scholarships, and related support for students in the US and Mexico, and even the opening of the state-level political system to enable Zacatecanos in the US to vote for governor and run for office in Zacatecas (Moctezuma, 2015). Yrizar Barbosa (2008) argues that a key issue was the repatriation of the bodies of Mexicans who died in the US (Lestage, 2012). These state-level differences have emerged from and enhanced political competition, as political parties seek to engage migrants abroad and their families at home. It has created a kind of mirror image to "immigration federalism" (Rodriguez, 2017; Varsanyi, 2010) in the US. Where inaction by the US Congress on immigration reform has spurred a variety of state and local policies seeking to integrate or exclude immigrants, including the undocumented, in Mexico, state and local governments initially took the lead in creating programs for their migrants abroad. While the federal government has created several substantial diasporic bureaucracies, an *emigration federalism* remains in Mexico, created by the variation in state and local policies and capacities to engage with their migrants abroad.

The seriousness of Mexico's intent can be measured in the progressive institutionalization of this work. From a small program started in the mid-1990s, Mexico's federal diasporic bureaucracies have grown and spanned four presidential terms, indicating that they aren't special projects but part of the government's central mission. Moreover, the training among consular staff has substantially changed, from a previous era's focus on international institutions like the UN to one including substantial training in migration-related work and scholarship covering transnational communities, migration, and remittances. The Mexican Consulate network in the US has grown to some 50 consulates in 25 states today (González Gutiérrez, 1999). This increased capacity has enabled the Mexican government to do more work with its diaspora than many other countries. Mexico has created or expanded several institutions through its Secretary of Foreign Affairs, including the Program for Mexican Communities Abroad in the mid-1990s and the creation of the Institute for Mexicans Abroad, or IME, in 2003, whose job it was to cultivate these ties. The Consultative Council of the Institute for Mexicans Abroad, or CCIME, was formed at the same time, with the goal of creating a space for immigrant leaders to be chosen by their peers to represent their interests to the IME and the Mexican government. Scholarship on IME and CCIME discusses motivations for and results of these programs (Alarcón, 2006; Délano, 2010, 2011; Délano & Yrizar Barbosa, 2017), but for this project's purposes, they clearly constitute diasporic bureaucracies.

Promoting knowledge of and access to health care among immigrants has been one of the most successful and least controversial areas of work for these Mexican diasporic bureaucracies. Mexico has had a National Health Week for 15 years, the Health Initiative of the Americas (HIA), set up in 2001 with the University of California–Berkeley School of Public Health to provide "action-oriented research" and "scientific-based activities to inform and influence policy changes," addressing the conditions of Latino populations and US–Mexico migration flows (Health, 2017). Mexico has set up Health Windows (HW, or Ventanillas de Salud) at all its US consulates, and implemented other work wherein local consulates partner with hospitals or other health-oriented institutions to promote better health in immigrant communities. These projects include campaigns against diabetes or Alzheimer's, as well as blood-pressure and blood-sugar screenings and referrals (Gambetta, 2012).[6]

Recent studies trace the history and increasing institutionalization of health policies toward Mexicans in the US. This institutionalization has run parallel to the consolidation of the Mexican consular network (*red consular*). As early as 1943, the creation of institutions like the US–Mexico Border Health Association and the Field Office of Panamerican Health Organization (Organización Panamericana de Salud, OPS) in El Paso, Texas (see also Border Health Commission, 2011), promoted such efforts (Salgado et al., 2012). Salgado and colleagues report that in 1990, the Mexican government offered health insurance for families under the name "IMSS Migrantes." In 2001, the Secretary of Health and Human Services of the US and the Mexican Secretary (Ministry) of Health created the United States–Mexico Border Health Commission (BHS). Furthermore, in 2004, BHS was designated a Public International Organization by Executive Order, with the mission of providing "international leadership to optimize health and quality of life along the US–México border" (U.S.–Mexico, n.d.). By 2009, Délano (2011) had identified 40 consulates in the US with HW; in 2016, there were 53 such HW, one in each consulate plus three "mobile" HW (Délano, 2018).[7]

State-level programs promoting the health of Mexicans in the US also emerged. Yrizar Barbosa (2008, p. 139) reports that in 2000, about a dozen Mexican state governments pledged (in the *Declaratoria de Puebla*) to "implement health campaigns" toward their populations in the US (pp. 75–76). Since 2001–2002, state officials from Michoacán have further participated in a Binational Health Week (BHW, Semana Binacional de Salud) in Los Angeles, California. However, some of these efforts are "paper programs" doing symbolic work but possessing little capacity to get work done. In 2007, the budget for Michoacán's State Program on Health for Migrants was about 12,350 MX pesos (less than US$1,200 at the time).

The government of Puebla has had a state-level office for Migrants Abroad for over a decade, and sometimes sought to do health programs, but the budget has varied. Its most important work has been to establish two Mi Casa Es Puebla locations, its official state offices, in NYC and Passaic, NJ. These offices serve as community centers promoting access to many services, including local, US-based health care, and also offer concrete help, such as issuing Mexican birth certificates for youth applying for Deferred Action for Childhood Arrivals (DACA).

Given this history, the SP research project we conducted in NY can be seen as an outgrowth of Mexico's work over the previous two decades as an innovator in state–diaspora relations. SP staff working with us on this study wanted to know how much Mexican immigrants in NY knew about SP, and if they could be urged to use it when they returned to Mexico—or at least encourage their families in Mexico to use it.

Toward this end, we posited three theories of action in our project. The first was to mobilize recent immigrants who were likely to return to Mexico because their families were there, and who were in NY only for a short stint to make money and return to Mexico. The second was to get long-term immigrants whose families had remained in Mexico to encourage those staying in their home country to use SP. The third was to encourage immigrants, those who migrated regularly between NY and Mexico as well as the long-term-settled in NY, to use SP when in Mexico to visit their relatives.

A larger issue involves the evaluation of these programs. Mexico usually evaluates its programs by presenting data on how many people attended or used them—e.g., how many people asked a question at the Health Windows? This offers a useful measure of activity but not of effect (Délano, 2018). How much do these programs promote the larger goals they seek to promote—to foster fuller integration and closer links with Mexico and serve the in-between needs of migrants who live in the US but have family in Mexico and who need support? We will return in Chapter 4 to this perennial question in evaluation research.

Social Marketing and Communication

Our project examines how immigrants and community leaders understood SP to develop approaches and language about the program that could ensure better comprehension and use. Our research from the first part of this book showed that public service promotions can change how immigrants think about the program. As will be detailed, our public service promotions increased knowledge of SP by 23%, and many migrants reported positive experiences with the program in Mexico, especially for relatives living in the country. While the first part of our project was primarily survey-based and sought to document the level of knowledge about SP among immigrants in NYC – and the factors that affect that level of knowledge – the latter part of this book focuses on *how* immigrants and their leaders understood or misunderstood SP and proposes strategies that SP and similar programs could use to promote more positive, accurate narratives about such health care initiatives in immigrant communities.

Our project applies an overarching "social marketing" strategy with immigrant populations. Social marketing is one of the most established approaches to developing or redeveloping public initiatives and is currently used by nonprofits, cities, and other public agencies across the planet, such as the World Health Organization, the US's National Institute for Child Health and Human Development, and the Centers for Disease Control and Prevention (Andreasen, 2005; Weinreich, 2010). Lee and Kotler (2016) clarify that "social marketing principles and techniques are most often used to improve public health, prevent injuries, protect the environment, increase involvement in the community and enhance financial well-being" (p. 33). Social marketing has been used to conceive, implement, and evaluate public campaigns, especially in domestic and transnational public health initiatives (Cheng, Kotler, & Lee, 2009; French et al., 2010; Harvey, 1999; Hastings, 2007; Lefebvre, 2009; Llanos-Zavalaga et al., 2004; Lovett, 2011; Rice & Robinson, 2013; Siegel & Donor, 1998; Smith, 2003). More on social marketing in general can be found in Kotler and Lee (2009), McKenzie-Mohr and Smith (2011), and Smith (2002).

For years, the social marketing literature has been replete with efforts to improve public health. Examples include Peru's campaign to reduce tuberculosis, Tokyo's movement to increase breast-cancer-screening rates, the organization NetMark's sustainable malaria-prevention efforts in Africa, Pakistan's family-planning initiatives, and India's initiatives to reduce diarrheal disease (Lee & Kotler, 2011; other research includes Asgedom, 2015; Lee & Kwak, 2012; Lovejoy & Saxton, 2012; Magro, 2012; Sabogal & Cordingley-Klein, 1999; Sugarman et al., 2011; Williams & Kumanyika, 2003). It is thus an appropriate framework for examining *how* immigrants and their leaders understand or misunderstand SP and for constructing new strategies that SP and similar programs can use to fashion more effective communication with their priority audiences.[8]

The social marketing and communication approaches applied in this book both critique and move us beyond many common ideas about how communication and outreach best work. Communication shouldn't be made into a "caricature of quick formulae and predetermined action, dissemination materials and media, and clever messages" that have remained the largely unreflective, staple approaches of many governments and agencies (Waisbord, 2015, pp. 155–156). The colossal waste of public funds spent by initiatives like the US government's over $1 billion National Youth Antidrug Media Campaign underscore the importance of this point. Evaluations of that campaign either showed no effects on youth beliefs and behavior around drug use, or potential "boomerang effects," where the campaign increased the very problems it sought to decrease (Hornik, 2013, p. 44). Social marketing and evidence-based work in communication hence take a multifaceted approach to change, drawing from and working with fields such as health communication, which use applied research and established theories that consider "the multicausality of social problems and recommend multilevel interventions" at individual, organizational, and policy levels (Waisbord, 2015, pp. 148–149).

We sought to promote health outcomes at the level of populations, which means aligning broader community action with communication strategies, not just throwing paid advertising at problems (Dorfman & Wallack, 2013, p. 337). Rather than appealing to intuition or tradition (Manheim, 2011), effective campaigns should incorporate long-standing theories of communication into their frameworks. Why reinvent the wheel when so much is already known about how communication works? Particularly in health communication, the value of basing government or organizational goals on a number of established communication concepts and frameworks continues to be supported in practice (Buller et al., 2013, p. 198). All the strategies we recommend in this book follow from our original survey, interview, and focus-group research, discussed at length in the following chapters. This book hence addresses a need highlighted by scholars and practitioners of strategic communication: to work across disciplines, using grounded empirical research, and to make "nonrelativistic conjectures" about how international communication could and should work (Nothhaft, 2016, p. 69). In the second part of this book, our research with immigrant communities will be integrated with this work to draw lessons for similar campaigns and initiatives seeking to improve their public marketing and outreach strategies.

Notes

1 This book doesn't fully examine the larger political forces affecting the creation of SP, as Smith (2008) did with Mexican migrants' right to vote from abroad.

2 The official, rather unwieldy, title of this first funded study was "Estudio del Nivel de Información Sobre el Seguro Popular con Que Cuenta la Población Migrante Mexicana de la Ciudad de Nueva York, EE.UU"

("Study about the Amount of Information about Seguro Popular among the Mexican Migrant Population in New York City"). Please note that we present the most important findings and themes from our previous research in this book. The original research report can be referred to for further details (Smith & Seguro Popular Team, 2012).

3 This change was preceded by a 2001 pilot program, Health for All (Salud para Todos), implemented in Aguascalientes, Campeche, Colima, Jalisco, and Tabasco (Uribe, Rodríguez, & Agudelo, 2013).

4 The Oportunidades program represented a major social-policy expansion and shift, changing the focus from treating poverty to longer-term changes enhancing incentives for families to invest in human capital, such as the education of their children.

5 We're aware of the analytical differences between migrants, immigrants, and emigrants, or what Waldinger (2015) identifies as a "paradox" in how societies of origin (sending country) and destination identify these populations differently. In this book, we decided to stick with the term "immigrants" because our perspective is from the society of destination (reception country).

6 At least since 1990, the Mexican government has developed health policies and programs targeting its nationals abroad (e.g., a binational program targeting United Farm Workers) (García-Acevedo, 1996, p. 140). By 2009, 40 consulates in the US had Health Windows, a program "designed to provide information on preventive health to persons who visit the Mexican consulates" (Délano, 2011, p. 212). More recently, the Program for Migrant Health (Programa para Salud Migrante)—a component of the National Program on Health 2007–2012—listed four objectives: (i) strengthen multilateral and bilateral ties; (ii) consolidate the Binational Health Weeks; (iii) promote SP among migrants, tapping on the HW; and (iv) improve the repatriation of sick Mexican immigrants (Salgado et al., 2012). In a visit to NYC (June 7–8, 2016), officials from the Mexican Secretary of Health and the Secretary of Foreign Affairs declared in a public statement that they were on a working visit with the intention to "promote the health services offered by the Government of the Republic to promote the integration of the Hispanic and Mexican-American communities in the United States" (IME, 2016: Boletín Especial Lazos #1672, June 8).

7 Salgado et al. (2012) situate the origin of the Binational Health Weeks in 2001 with the Health Initiative of the Americas and—in addition to the Health Windows or SP programs for migrant families (since 2010 and migrant children since 2011, in collaboration with DIF, or the National System for Integral Family Development)—they mention the following health programs for migrants: Programa de Repatriación de Connacionales Enfermos (by the ministries of Foreign Affairs and Health); and Programa Vete Sano, Regresa Sano (started in 2001 by the Health Ministry). These researchers also identified the Program for Migrant Health (Programa para Salud Migrante) as part of the National Program on Health in 2007–2012. In 2015, the Mexican Health Secretary/ Ministry, via two offices (Dirección General de Relaciones Internacionales and Dirección General Adjunta Para la Salud del Migrante), listed seven health programs for the Mexican migrant population: HW, the Program for the Repatriation of Sick Conationals, BHWs, Programa de

Investigación en Migración y Salud (PIMSA), Programa de Trabajadores Agrícolas Temporales (PTAT), Modulos de Atención Integral de Salud para Connacionales Repatriados, and BHS/CSF. For additional studies stating the challenges of binational health in North America, such as the initiatives Salud Migrante and Medicare in Mexico, or the most recent efforts to address the link between undocumented migration in the US or specifically in NYC, see Vargas Bustamante et al. (2012), Rodríguez, Young, and Wallace (2015), and Barrios-Paoli (2015). At least since the late 1990s, those born outside the US are least likely to possess health-insurance coverage (Reed, 1998).

8 At the same time, we will apply interdisciplinary research on communication strategy to SP. Public campaigns that don't use such approaches (incorporating applied research and social-scientific knowledge on communication strategy) put themselves at a serious disadvantage in a cluttered and competitive information environment (Lanham, 2006; Manheim, 2011; Smith, 2012).

2 What Do Mexican Immigrants in New York Know and Think about Seguro Popular?

With assistance from Wei Ting Lu, Eduardo Peñaloza, Julio César García Torres, and Angelo Cabrera

The first Seguro Popular (SP) research project sought to discover how much Mexicans in New York knew about the program, what factors influenced that knowledge, and to see if they or their families might use it. This research uncovered the surprising finding that Mexicans in NY were rejecting SP because of how it was being framed as a social right, but that they might embrace it if it were framed differently, as an insurance policy. This finding led SP to commission, via CIDE (Centro de Investigación y Docencia Económica; a higher-education institution in Mexico), a second study, which we present in Chapter 3 (Smith et al., 2012).

Research Goals and Strategy

Our research goals in the first SP research project were threefold: to measure how much Mexican immigrants in NY knew about the SP program; to conduct public service promotions (interventions, but of a particular kind, as we discuss below) increasing knowledge about it; and to measure the effects of these promotions, with the goal of promoting its use. Our research strategy followed what we would call an *observational before-after, rolling public service promotion-assessment* model, which was better than other models for several reasons. We conducted a baseline, or "before," survey of a stratified convenience sample of Mexican immigrants in NY from August through September 2011, against which we measured the effects of our several, subsequent public service promotions. The sample purposely included roughly an equal number of men and women, and was done inside the consulate waiting room and outside it, in parks or neighborhoods, to avoid the bias that sampling from one place might introduce. We also completed interviews to more deeply understand knowledge and use of SP.

We conducted our surveys inside and outside the Mexican Consulate. Inside the consulate, we used the waiting room, through which some 300–500 people pass daily. Outside the consulate, we went independently to public places where Mexicans congregate (e.g., soccer and baseball fields, Mexican neighborhoods), and piggybacked on the Mexican Consulado sobre Ruedas, or Consulate on Wheels. By piggybacking, we mean going to events with naturally occurring large concentrations of Mexicans, so we could distribute a lot of literature in a short time (Smith, 2006, 2012). A Consulate on Wheels involves consular personnel performing their services at a site removed from the consulate building in NY—at a community organization, church, or school—including getting consular IDs or Mexican passports. This is a further enactment of Mexico's diasporic bureaucracy strategy that seeks to engage and develop local leaders with whom the consulate can then work (Délano, 2014, p. 98). We speculated that people going to the consulate to get documents would more likely be undocumented than those approached in public places, but our surveys didn't bear this out, so we have broken down the sample in our analysis below.

Carefully describing our research design and methods clarifies the analytical purchase of our research questions. We describe our approach as an observational before-after, rolling public service promotion-assessment design to accurately describe it and to avoid the confusion that might result from using the language of more experimental or quasi-experimental research designs. Experimental research designs enable researchers to assess the effect of a "treatment" or an "intervention" on an outcome because the researcher controls the treatment or intervention *and* the assignment of who gets the treatment (the treatment group) or does not (the control group) and can reasonably assume or show no difference between the groups. Under these conditions, researchers' claims that the treatment caused the change in outcome are strengthened, supporting a claim of measuring causal effect and inference. Quasi-experimental research doesn't control who is assigned to treatment and control groups but can identify who is in each group and plausibly argue that a distribution in a group is random or as-if random, enabling causal inference (Dunning, 2012; Winship & Morgan, 1999).

Practical and ethical considerations, including the goals of the study, made a formal experimental approach impossible. First, the Mexican government, which funded the study and provided for research to be conducted at the consulate, made clear that it couldn't selectively withhold information on SP from some and not other migrants. Second, it wasn't possible to control who did and did not get exposed to the public service promotions we designed—and ethically and logically, withholding this information from some potential users of SP would have been against the goal of encouraging more use of those programs. Third, given the utter lack of knowledge of SP, we had to explain the program briefly to those surveyed to get them to participate, thus affecting their knowledge of it (the outcome in this chapter, discussed below). We hence avoid the language of "treatment"/"intervention," "control," and "causal inference."

One can legitimately use *logical inference* (if not experimental causal inference) to draw conclusions about how changes observed in data on outcomes (here, knowledge of SP) gathered before and after public service promotions (or similar nonexperimental changes) happened, however—especially with both quantitative and qualitative data and when the analytical goals of the project don't require experimental causal inference (Brady, 2005; Smith, 2019). If the goal of the project had been to evaluate the efficacy of a new cancer drug, a formal experiment would be needed. But the goal here was to assess how much people know about SP, and then promote awareness and use of it in any way possible.

We used seven public service promotions: (1) distributing a pamphlet showing two kitchen workers discussing SP (Figure 1.1 in Chapter 1); (2) a text message sent to 30,000 Mexicans' cell phones by the Mexican consulate; (3) four appearances to talk about SP on radio programs, with 25,000 listeners, conducted by the Mexican Consulate; (4) coverage on Spanish-language television; (5) a banner on websites of key Mexican-led and Mexican-serving organizations and their Facebook pages; (6) a video about SP running in the Mexican Consulate waiting room, through which 300–500 persons pass daily, and also on a special website we developed for this project; and (7) an explanation of the program to those surveyed by the researchers, which we coded as a public service promotion when we realized we had to explain the benefit of the program to get people to participate. (Our coding differentiated between those who already knew about SP, and those who only came to know about it when invited to do the survey. This innovation captures data to measure a Hawthorne Effect, as per Smith (2019).[1]

These public service promotions were completed on a rolling basis, described below, over the course of the project. We use logical inference to describe the effects of those promotions. Our data show very low knowledge of SP at the start of the project, which increased strongly by the end, and that knowledge of SP (the outcome) was significantly associated with specific factors, controlling for others. While we refrain from making formal causal inferences, we logically infer that our public service promotions increased knowledge of this program. We can ask the commonsense, counterfactual question of what else might have caused these increases. Even if the new knowledge that people gained wasn't from seeing such promotions but from someone telling them about them, the increase is still happening because of those interventions and could still help people learn about health insurance. We return to this issue later.

While continuing to do surveys, we conducted public service promotions in three phases. In the first public service promotion, between mid-September and late October 2011, we piggybacked on the consulate's outreach and local events with large concentrations of NY's Mexican population—e.g., at soccer games, Mexican Independence Day events, or community organizations such as Masa (Mexican American Students' Alliance) in the Bronx or La Unión in Brooklyn. We disseminated information about SP using traditional face-to-face approaches (Cousineau, Stevens, & Farias, 2010; collaborated with Spanish-language news and other media; and used social media like Facebook and participating organization websites.

The second phase involved an ongoing public service promotion, where we continued to distribute SP materials at the consulate, had community organizations disseminate materials more broadly, and anonymously interviewed community leaders and immigrants reporting problems with SP. The third phase began after mid-November 2011, lasted through February 2012, and included posting our own, expanded web-based materials on banners in community organizations' websites and placing posters in their facilities, running a video loop at the consulate, and doing more interviews. We conducted 849 surveys in total, and about 40 interviews, including repeat interviews, which were part of our attempts to resolve issues that emerged on SP's use by our interviewees. These mixed methods enabled us to use statistical inference and process-based data (interviews, mainly) in analyzing outcomes, how they came about, and how future outreach to immigrants could be designed.

Observational before-after policy promotion (or, as it is often termed, intervention) studies range in size, complexity, and duration. The norm is for larger-scale, experimental or quasi-experimental studies focusing on existing data, using huge samples that enable an analysis to meet or approximate experimental standards. One study used an existing, ongoing survey of more than 40,000 military personnel over a six-year period to gauge the effects of deployment on sleep and the well-being of veterans (Seelig et al., 2010). Other studies gauged the changing stress levels for those qualifying for disability benefits before and after their disability hearings (Overland et al., 2008), or changes in the use of health programs after the introduction of copayments. Cousineau et al. (2010) evaluated the effectiveness of outreach programs seeking to promote enrollment in a new insurance program for low-income people in California using large-scale interventions and enrollment data for the entire state of California over a six-year period. Such large-scale studies offer the benefit of statistical inference in discerning relationships among variables, but are more limited by their difficulties in discerning complex causality. In many cases, investigators identify statistically significant correlations but must speculate without process-level data on what these correlations mean. Moy and Chabner (2011) evaluated the effect of the Affordable Care Act on the use of cancer treatments among vulnerable populations, focusing on the role of navigators in helping patients get care. Others have done similar studies focusing on promoting health care use among immigrants, including via mosques to promote heart health (Bader et al., 2006).

A second kind of before-after study, a "smallball" study, seeks to determine the effects of policy changes at a particular organization, usually over the life cycle of the project under study (Friedman, 2005; Olney, 2005; Ottoson & Green, 2005). Such interventions and studies don't use the same logic of analysis or standards of evidence as large, randomized studies but offer insights into *how* particular programs work. They usually rely on smaller samples and more process-oriented data and evaluation, such as interviews and focus groups, or data internal to the organization about the new program (Friedman, 2005; Robson, 2010; Small, 2009; Smith, 2006). They're usually shorter in duration than larger, randomized projects. A disadvantage is that conclusions thus reached cannot be generalized to a larger population. However, such process-oriented data and analysis often provide actionable insights that organizations can use in designing or reforming their own policies. Our research design included elements of both larger and smallball studies. Our before-after evaluation design was strengthened by using the same outreach venues and methods to ensure that we contacted the same kinds of people throughout the study. Our study showed significant effects to our public service promotion over a three-month period, and we gained insight into the institutional contexts that immigrant families face in making health care decisions.

Primary, Time-Limited Public Service Promotion

Our first targeted, time-limited public service promotion strategy sought to capitalize on two naturally occurring sets of events that the Mexican population in NY attends: Mexican Independence Day and Binational Health Weeks. From mid-September to late October, we went to celebrations of Mexican independence organized by the consulate and community leaders, e.g., a parade in East Harlem, and distributed literature on SP while also doing surveys and interviews. We placed an ad for our website (explained below) in *Diario de México* during Binational Health Weeks, and our SP research project was featured in a news report by Marisa Cespedes on Televisa (in Mexico and NY), wherein the anchor interviewed project staff and an immigrant whose relative had benefited from SP. Univision and Telemundo told how to enroll in SP through their regular features *Mi México a Su Servicio, El Informador,* and *Pregúntale a Tu Consulado,* as well as CUNY's "Sí Se Puede" website. We distributed more than 2,000 pieces of literature to immigrants throughout these events. We talked about SP four times in a weekly one-hour radio program, *Mexicano, Pregúntale a Tu Consulado,* which has approximately 25,000 listeners, and created a website for SP in NY (www.seguropopularny.com; no longer active) offering basic information about SP and links to SP's main website (www.seguro-popular.gob.mx) for further information.

Second and Third Public Service Promotions

We developed the NY SP website more during the second, continued public service promotion, through February 2012. We added two testimonials of immigrants to the site. Since people tend to remember emotionally compelling, specific information more than abstract policy statements or statistical reasoning (Zillman, 2006), we used two exemplary videos. Mayra, a young woman from Puebla, tells visitors that she only recently learned of SP and that her family in Mexico is enrolled, so she doesn't have to worry anymore. Humberto, a young immigrant from Tlaxcala whose wife in Mexico just had a baby, tells visitors that SP "took good care" (*le atendieron muy bien*) of his wife, that the birth didn't cost them anything, and that SP's "program is too good" (*un programa demasiado bueno*). Some community organizations even put SP's site up on their website banner, making the stories of Humberto and Mayra and information about SP accessible to their constituents.

We set up a video loop of Mayra's and Humberto's testimonials in the Mexican Consulate waiting room, where 300–500 Mexican immigrants often wait 2–2.5 hours to be helped daily, giving them ample time to watch one-minute video clips 10–15 times on four televisions distributed across two floors of the consulate waiting room. Visitors also learned about the consulate's Programa Ventanilla de Salud (Health Window Program), where they could preregister for SP and even link this preregistration to their families in Mexico.[2] Prior research (Cousineau et al., 2010) confirms that this type of individual counseling effectively promotes registration and use of health-insurance programs.

Toward the end of our study period, we added to our continuing public service promotions a third public service promotion using other media. We advertised three more days in *Diario de México*, with pictures of Mayra and Humberto and our website address. *El Especialito*, a Spanish-language Mexican newspaper in NJ and NY, featured SP and our project. Other community organizations placed our video clips on their website banners and put up posters advertising SP.[3] We sent email blasts, September–December 2011, on five weekly bulletins to 13,252 email addresses on the consular list, with information about SP and the telephone number for the Health Window. Several text blasts reached some 30,000 mobile phones of Mexican immigrants, and Twitter feeds with SP information were targeted to a list of 1,030 enlisted followers. Of the 849 surveys completed during our initial project, 729 were from early September to mid-November, and another 120 were completed during this last public service promotion phase after mid-November 2011 through February 2012.

The Mexican Population in New York and Our Sample

This project generated a sample broadly reflective of the actual population. Figure 2.1 is a map showing results of our loading the 2005–2009 American Community Survey (ACS) data on the Mexican population distribution in NY with the zip codes of those surveyed (red dots) for this project, using GIS. The ACS, generated by the Census Bureau, is used by most demographers for detailed analysis, especially later in a decade, as the last census's data becomes outdated. The significant overlap between our data and ACS data shows that we captured the Mexican population's geographic distribution, including the "Little Mexicos" emerging in East Harlem and Washington Heights; Mott Haven, South Bronx; Jackson Heights, Queens; and Sunset Park, Brooklyn. This surprising dispersal makes sense not only because it follows some of the subway lines (Smith, 2006) but because these neighborhoods have affordable housing (Yrizar Barbosa, Smith, & Reed, 2016). The overall Mexican origin population in NY has increased in official census estimates, from 58,410 in 1990 to 187,259 in 2000, to 342,699 in 2010 (Bergad, 2013). Considering undercounts, these numbers were likely about 100,000 in 1990, about 450,000 in 2010, and more than 500,000 today.[4]

This project's sample shows similar state-of-origin data with three other large-scale surveys that the first author has directed since 1993, ranging from 450 to 849 persons. All the surveys show that immigrants from Puebla constitute the single biggest segment of the population (42% in 2012, down from 47% in 1993), while others increased, including surrounding states such as Guerrero and Oaxaca (together increasing from 18% in 1993 to 21% in 2012 of the total), and from Mexico City (Distrito Federal, or DF) and Estado de México (together increasing from 11% to 14% in the same period).[5] The consistency in these estimates lends support to the validity of numbers offered in the current survey.

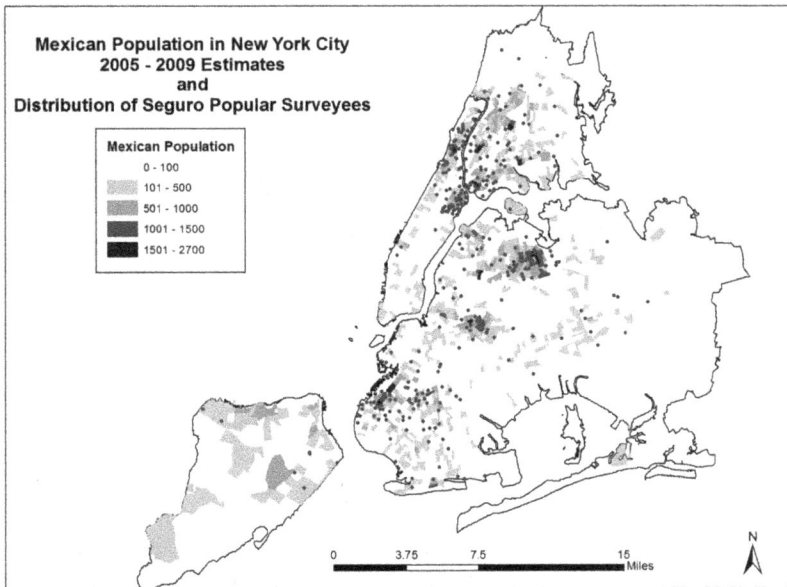

Mexican Population in New York City
2005 - 2009 Estimates
and
Distribution of Seguro Popular Surveyees

Mexican Population
0 - 100
101 - 500
501 - 1000
1001 - 1500
1501 - 2700

0   3.75   7.5   15 Miles

N

Source: 2005-2009 American Community Survey 5-year Estimates

Figure 2.1 Mexican Population in New York City (2005–2009) and Distribution of 2012 SP Surveys.

Our overall sample was 52% male and 48% female, a deliberate over-sampling compared with the 166 men and 100 women the ACS showed in NY's overall Mexican-born population. The mean age was 36.2 years old, with 8.8 years of education (more than the six years found by Valdes de Montano & Smith in 1994), with 11.7 years living in the US. Only 37% had returned to Mexico to visit, probably because of legal immigration status.

Some 32% of surveys were pre-public service promotion baselines (before September 16, 2011), 29% were done during the first public service promotions (September 16, 2011–October 14, 2011), 25% during the second, continuing public service promotion (October 14, 2011–November 4, 2011), and 14% during the third, final public service promotion (November 4, 2011–February 2012). Over half (51%) the surveys were conducted in the consulate's waiting room, while 40% were completed outside it (through Consulates on Wheels), at community organizations, or other public places. Some 9% were completed in Red Hook Park in early September.

Our sample included mainly long-term undocumented residents. Only 4.9% reported being US citizens, 9.1% permanent residents, and 2.4% other visa holders. We calculated undocumented status in two ways. The first estimate includes those who directly reported expired visas or undocumented status, which yielded 79% undocumented and 21% documented participants (excluding those who didn't report a status). Second, we presumed those who didn't answer questions regarding legal status to be undocumented, yielding an 84% undocumented rate, overall, and a 16% documented rate. Either way, this was a strong majority. Our respondents were not newcomers. While 22% had been in the US for five years or less, 30% had 6–10 years, 20% had 11–15 years, 17% had 16–20 years, and 11% had over 20 years.[6]

This strong relationship of legal status to duration of time in the US directly reflects US policy. The last main large-scale opportunity for undocumented people to legalize was during the so-called amnesty program of the Immigration Reform and Control Act of 1986 (IRCA; see Waisanen, 2012). This legalization program ran through autumn 1998 and legalized more than three million people, including a large portion of Mexicans in NY (Smith, 2006). What followed was what Smith (2013) called a "Moratorium Period" that lasted until President Obama signed his Executive Order for Deferred Action for Childhood Arrivals (DACA) in 2012, a few months after the completion of this research. Our data document the percentage of undocumented people as 90%–93% for persons who have been in the US 0–15 years.

Absent obstacles, one would expect the numbers to fall more quickly. The percentage falls to only 73% with 16–20 years in the US and doesn't fall under half (46%) until one has over 20 years in the United States. Immigrants who legalized under IRCA received a road to legal status and citizenship, which meant they reunified their families through the early to mid-1990s, 15–20 or more years before our survey in 2012 (Alanís Enciso & Alarcón Acosta, 2016). The relationship between time in the US and legal status hence derives from US immigration policy. US immigration policy's emphasis on making border crossing harder (which also made it more dangerous) changed incentives away from the dominant circular migration pattern of the previous quarter-century and toward increased settlement and full family reunification—even for the undocumented—boosting that population from about 3 million to about 12 million in the early 2000s (Massey, Durand, & Malone, 2002).

Accessing Medical Insurance in the US

The accessibility of medical insurance by Mexican immigrants and their families in NY is relevant to their interest in the SP program. Children and adults have completely different stories regarding health care (see Figure 2.2). Some 73% of adults don't have any health insurance in the US, while 16% had it through public programs (such as the Health and Hospitals Corporation [HHC]), and only 5% through work or a union, 2% via private insurance, and 1% via relatives.

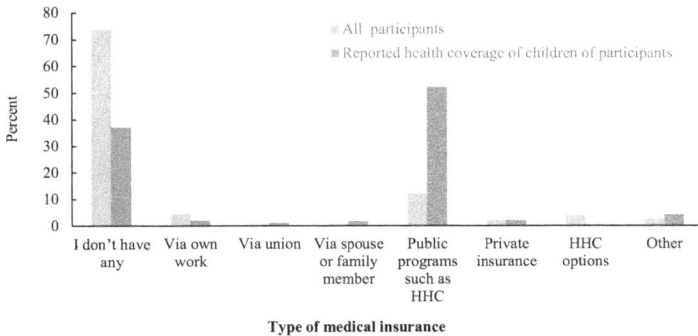

N = 849; with children in the U.S. N = 635.

Figure 2.2 Medical Coverage for Mexicans in New York and Their Children, by Type of Insurance.

In contrast, a majority—52%—of those surveyed reported that their children had public health insurance and another 10% were insured through other options. Children have greater access to insurance because many are US citizens by birth, affording them more access than their parents, and NY State's Child Health Plus program offers free or low-cost health insurance to all low-income New Yorkers under the age of 21. This NY State entitlement program isn't restricted by legal status because it's not a federal program.

The Effects of Our Public Service Promotion

The SP research project's public service promotions, described above, sought to increase exposure to and conversations about SP. We assessed our public service promotions by examining relations between several variables, including level of knowledge about SP. In Figure 2.3, we report frequencies on a question from our survey, "Did you know you can get access to medical insurance for yourself and your family through Seguro Popular?" We report these results in two ways to resolve a catch-22 in doing survey-based research. To initially get people to complete the survey, we had to explain what SP was. With interest piqued, most would then do the 15–20-minute survey. A data issue was that many who hadn't known of SP would then come to know it through the surveyor and answer yes when asked the question. We had effectively changed the nature of the phenomenon under study by our attempt to measure it (Jones, 1992). So in Figure 2.3, we count answers indicating that the subject knew about SP, but only through the surveyor, as "no"

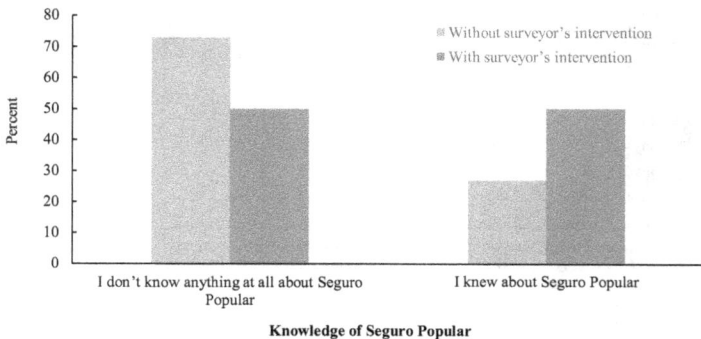

N = 841; eight cases missing out of 849 participants.

Figure 2.3 Knowledge of SP for Mexicans in New York, by Surveyor's Intervention.

answers, i.e., "I do not know about SP." In Figure 2.3, we counted all answers that the subject knew about SP, but only through the surveyor, as "yes" answers, i.e., as positive for non-detailed knowledge of SP. By reporting both measures, we captured and can disentangle the effect of the surveyor on knowledge of SP.

Figure 2.3 shows that 73% of informants knew nothing about SP, while 27% knew something about it (23.1% knew something about it, and only 3.9% knew one or more details, which we combined into one measure). Figure 2.3 also reports how many surveyed persons knew about SP through the surveyor. It shows that 49.9% knew nothing, while 50.1% knew something (but only 3.9% knew any detail of SP, included in the 50.1%). Hence, the surveyor's explanation/ public service promotion immediately boosted the awareness of SP by 23%, from 27% to 50%.

Table 2.1 reports logistic regression results for a model where the dependent variable is a recoded version of our question about knowledge of SP, recoded hereafter as "yes" for any level of knowledge. This model considers the effects of sex, age, years of education, years in the US, legal status, having ever visited Mexico since one's arrival in the US, and various dates of the public service promotion. Sex is coded as male = 1, female = 0; age is a continuous variable coded as a whole numeral, as is years in the US. Legal status is coded as 1 = undocumented status reported directly and 0 = documented, which includes any form of legal status, including US citizenship. Having ever visited Mexico is coded as 1 = having visited, and 0 = not having visited.[7]

The primary public service promotion piggybacked on the events that the consulate had already organized around Mexican Independence Day, on and around September 16, and the Binational Health Weeks, which began September 29 and ran through October 14, as well as the creation of a website for SP in NY, coverage on Televisa, and distribution of SP literature at public events and community organizations. We hence treat them as two parts of a single public service promotion period. The period after October 14, 2011–November 4, 2011 was a second continuing public service promotion, where we weren't piggybacking on consular events, but we had ongoing dissemination about SP through consular radio programs, through pamphlets and information sessions of the Health Window, and through providing pamphlets and other information at community organizations. The final or third public service promotion period was November 4, 2011–February 28, 2012, and included renewed advertisements through *El Diario La Prensa*, posting our video materials on community-organization banners, the video loop in the consular waiting room, placing posters in community organizations, and dissemination of SP literature at the consulate and community organizations.

Table 2.1 Summary of Logistic Regression Analysis for Variables Predicting Knowledge on Seguro Popular for Mexicans in New York ($N = 849^a$)

| | Model (1) | | Model (2) | |
| | Immigrant Experience | | Intervention | |
Predictor	B	OR	B	OR
List Demographic Variables				
Sex (*women* = 1; *men* = 0)	0.253	1.288	0.275	1.317
Age	0.007	1.007	0.008	1.008
Education	0.017	1.018	0.027	1.027
List Immigrant Experience Variables				
Years in the US	−0.030**	0.970	−0.033**	0.968
Undocumented Status	−0.250	0.778	−0.199	0.820
(*Undocumented* = 1; *documented* = 0)^b				
Having Ever Visited Mexico	0.066	1.069	0.120	1.128
(*Yes* = 1; *No* = 0)				
List Intervention Variables				
9/16/11–10/14/11			0.543**	1.722
(*Before 9/16/11* = 0, as reference group)				
10/14/11–11/04/11			0.695***	2.004
(*Before 9/16/11* = 0, as reference group)				
After 11-4-11			1.049***	2.854
(*Before 9/16/11*= 0, as reference group)				
Constant	0.020		−0.628	
Pseudo R^2 (Nagelkerke)	0.16		0.056***	

Note: OR = odds ratio. * $p < 0.05$; **$p < 0.01$; ***$p < 0.001$.
a   Total number of respondents in the Seguro Popular Survey.
b   Undocumented status predictor is coded as 1 for undocumented and 0 for documented. Undocumented status includes those who reported that they were undocumented, who said that they had an expired visa, who did not want to answer, and whom the interviewer did not ask about their legal status. Reasons for this coding are explained in the text. Documented status includes those who are US citizens, visa holders, and permanent residents.

Surveys conducted before September 16, 2011, constituted the comparison group for all three public service promotions because during that period, we did no outreach or promotion of SP (beyond the public service promotion of the surveyors). Segmenting the sample into these groups sought to measure the public service promotions' effects over time. Our research shows that the effect of the public service promotions grew stronger over time and that more subjects were aware of SP the longer the public service promotion lasted. Theoretically, this is what one would expect.

In Table 2.1, the Model 1 regression equation shows that the only factor playing a significant role in knowledge of SP is the number of years in the US. The odds ratio of 0.97 in Model 1 shows that for each year in the US, one is 3% less likely to know about SP. Someone who was in the US for ten years thus had a 30% lower chance of knowing about SP. This makes sense, since someone with ten years in the US in 2012 had left in 2002, two years before SP began.

The Model 2 regression equation showed that years in the US still decreased the chances that one would know about SP, by a statistically significant 3.3%. It also showed that our public service promotions had a strong positive effect on knowledge of SP, which grew stronger over time. Those surveyed during the first public service promotion, September 16, 2011–October 14, 2011, had a 72% greater chance of knowing about SP than those surveyed before September 16. Those surveyed October 15, 2011–November 4, 2011 were twice as likely (2.0 log odds ratio) to know than those asked before September 6, 2011. And those contacted after November 4, 2011, were 2.85 times more likely to know than those asked before September 16, 2011. We were pleased with this result, which suggested that even relatively low-level public service promotions can have an important effect on knowledge about SP among Mexican immigrants.

We illustrate the effects of the public service promotion in Figure 2.4, showing the percentages of respondents who knew or did not know about SP before our public service promotions and between the other public service promotion dates. Some 61% of the respondents interviewed before the start of the first public service promotion didn't know about SP; this number declined steadily over the course of the project to 48% during the first public service promotion, to 44% during the continuing public service promotion, and 37.6% during the second public service promotion. Similarly, the percentage of people knowing about SP increased from 39%–52% to 56%–62% over the course of the project. These numbers reflect a statistically significant 13% increase in knowledge about SP over the course of the project.

We asked respondents *how* they had learned about SP—critical information in assessing how to promote knowledge about the program. The most frequent way—52% of all the people who knew about SP—was through the interviewer him or herself (see Figure 2.5). As discussed, approaching informants to do the survey required explaining SP enough to persuade them to participate in the survey. The next most important sources of knowledge were family or friends, at 24%; the Mexican Consulate, at 8%; television, 5%; other, 4%; and community

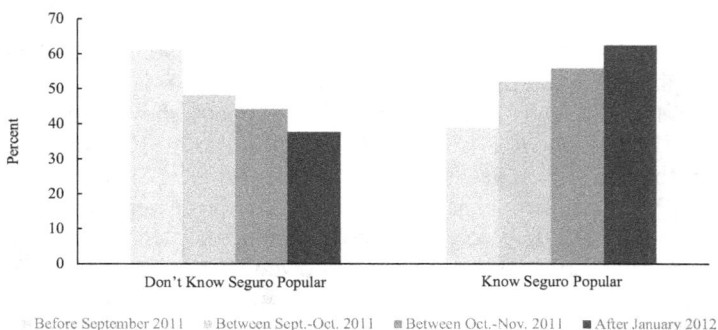

N = 841; eight cases missing out of 849 participants.

Figure 2.4 Knowledge of SP for Mexicans in New York, by Intervention Date.

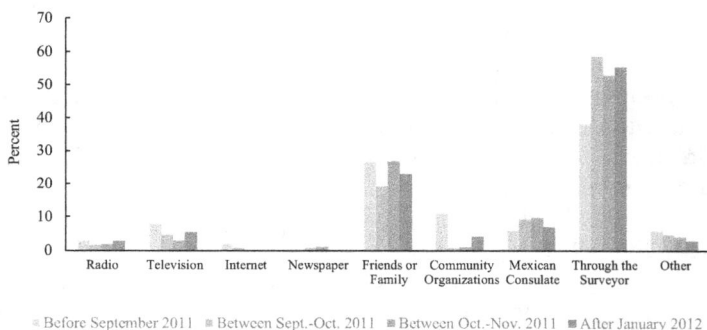

N = 410; includes 78 cases interviewed in Red Hook.

Figure 2.5 How Mexicans in New York Learned about SP, by Intervention Date.

organizations, 4%. These findings reflect the lack of prior awareness about SP among these NY immigrants and suggest that face-to-face contact is key in promoting knowledge of such programs, a finding that we'll build upon in the second part of this book. Similar research recognizes the utility of television, radio, newspapers, and, especially, social media, in doing such outreach or encouraging registration for an insurance program—e.g., in California (Cousineau et al., 2010). Given the lack of information about SP among Mexicans in NY prior to our project, these numbers can be construed as net gains, purchased relatively cheaply.

Locating Possible and Actual Immigrant Family Beneficiaries

The Mexican government commissioned this study, believing that immigrants in the US would have relatives who qualified for SP and that they could be induced to encourage their relatives who hadn't yet done so to sign up. Hence, we asked other questions to determine if respondents had family members in Mexico who might qualify. This part of the survey was conversational, and our intent was to be both helpful and get accurate data. We asked respondents if they thought that they had qualifying relatives and would discuss who might qualify (see Table 2.2). Over half the total sample (54.8%) and nearly three-quarters (71.9%) of the valid percentage (i.e., those who actually answered it) for this question thought they had a family member in Mexico who qualified for SP. We asked respondents to identify which family members in Mexico might qualify. Some 60.9% of respondents believed that their parents in Mexico would qualify, followed by 22.8% naming children or others; 9.2%, a spouse; and 7.1%, grandparents. Because this question asked who they thought would qualify after the surveyor had explained SP to them, it can be seen as a relatively reliable indicator.

Answers to a further set of questions suggested that SP has been well used by those who knew about it but underused by the immigrant family population as a whole. For those who had previously heard of SP, we continued with questions about their own or their family's experiences of it. Only 106 out of 849 respondents had talked to a family member in Mexico about SP (see Table 2.2). Answers showed that 88, or 10.4%, of the total sample reported that a family member had used SP. Given that only 227 out of 849 (27%, as shown previously in Figure 2.3) subjects knew about SP without the surveyor's public service promotion, this was a surprisingly high number. It meant that 47% (106 of 227) of those who knew about SP before talking to the surveyor had talked to family members in Mexico about it. Moreover, while only 106 subjects had talked to someone in Mexico about SP, 88 of them (83%) had a family member who had used the program. These statistics suggest that as more families in Mexico use the program, it will become an active part of discussions with their immigrant relatives, increasing knowledge of the program. They also suggest that talking to immigrants about SP could increase knowledge and use of the program among families in Mexico with relatives who are international migrants. This finding pleased SP officials and echoed some of their original thinking in seeking to have this study completed.

Table 2.2 Mexicans in New York with Potentially Eligible Family Members for Seguro Popular

	Frequency	Percent	Valid Percent
Question #22: Do you have family who you think would be eligible for this (SP) coverage in Mexico?			
Yes	465	54.8	71.9
No	182	21.4	28.1
Answers to Q22	647	76.2	100.0
N/A	202	23.8	
All participants	849	100.0	
Question #23: After this explanation (of SP), do you think you have a family member who qualifies for SP?			
Spouse	48	5.7	9.2
Parents	318	37.5	60.9
Grandparents	37	4.4	7.1
Children or others	119	14.0	22.8
Answers to Q22	522	61.5	100.0
N/A	327	38.5	
All participants	849	100.0	
Question #24: Have you talked to a family member in Mexico about this program (SP)?			
Yes	106	12.5	23.2
No	350	41.2	76.8
Answers to Q24	456	53.7	100.0
N/A	393	46.3	
All participants	849	100.0	
Question #25: Has your family used this medical coverage (by SP)?			
Yes	88	10.4	64.7
No	48	5.7	35.3
Answers to Q25	136	16.0	100.0
N/A	713	84.0	
All participants	849	100.0	

Note: For further questions and details, see Seguro Popular in New York Survey in Appendix B.

Diaspora Questions

Two "diaspora questions" sought to gauge respondents' larger stance toward Mexico to see if that affected their knowledge or use of SP (see Figure 2.6). We asked respondents to agree or disagree with the statement "Mexico is concerned with the welfare of its migrants in the US." We asked immigrants their opinion on a five-point Likert scale: (1) disagree strongly, (2) disagree, (3) indifferent,

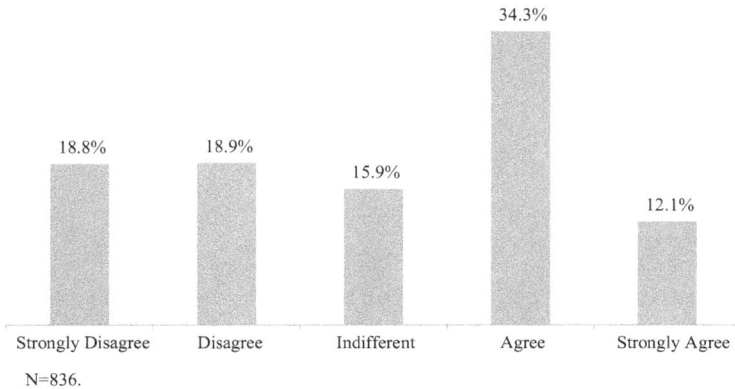

Figure 2.6 Opinion to Statement for Participants in SP Project in New York: "Mexico Is Concerned about Its Migrants in the United States."

(4) agree, and (5) agree strongly. Answers showed that less than a third of the sample held strong opinions (1 or 5). The majority held more mild or neutral opinions (2, 3, or 4). Interestingly, 46.4% of respondents thought that Mexico worries some of the time about its immigrants (4 and 5), while 37.7% disagreed to some degree (1 and 2). Given the widespread perception in the research literature and in public discussion that immigrants blame the political and economic climate of Mexico for their migration, this was an unanticipated finding.

Another question, "What opinion do you think Mexicans have about persons who migrate to the US?" (Figure 2.7), was answered through a three-point Likert scale: (1) negative, (2) indifferent, and (3) positive. Recent immigrants are more likely to believe that their counterparts in Mexico hold positive opinions of them than do those who migrated earlier. Only 8.5% of immigrants with 1–5 years in the US believed that Mexicans in Mexico held a negative opinion of them, while 56.5% thought that Mexicans in Mexico held a positive opinion. In contrast, of those in the US with 21-plus years, 15.9% thought that their compatriots in Mexico held negative opinions of immigrants, and 51.1% thought that they held positive opinions. These findings comport with previous research and opinions among community leaders that most long-term immigrants wouldn't think they were seen favorably in Mexico, or would themselves have a negative opinion about whether Mexico is concerned about its immigrants in the US.

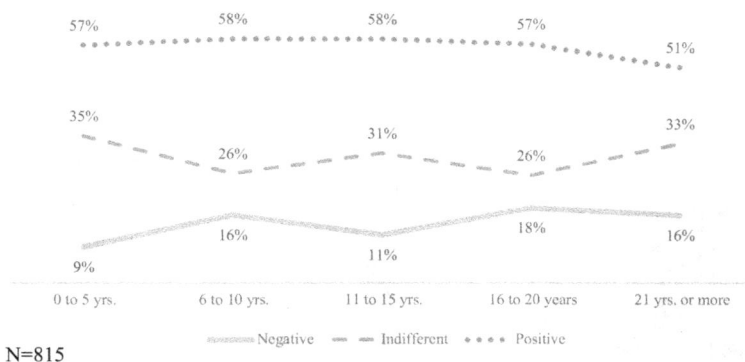

N=815

Figure 2.7 Participant Belief of Whether Mexicans Hold a Positive, Negative, or Indifferent Opinion of Emigrants, by Years in the United States.

Exploring the data, we found that people who knew about SP strongly agreed that Mexico is concerned about its immigrants abroad (15.5%), compared with those who didn't know (8.7%). A slightly higher percentage of those who strongly disagree that Mexico cares about its immigrants also know about SP (17.8% know; 15.2% don't know). We interpret these findings to mean that when people know that Mexico offers SP, they're more likely to feel it cares for its immigrants abroad; but if someone has a family member who has had a problem with SP, he or she is more likely to think that Mexico doesn't care about its immigrants abroad.

We can evaluate the effect of our public service promotions on respondents' beliefs about Mexico's concern for them. We analyzed how our public service promotions affected one's belief that the Mexican government is concerned about immigrant welfare abroad (see Table 2.3). The three public service promotions were statistically significant ($p < 0.05$), all increasing the likelihood that one would believe that Mexico is concerned about its immigrants abroad. Respondents surveyed September 16, 2011–October 14, 2011 were 86% more likely to believe that Mexico worried about its immigrants than those surveyed before the public service promotion (before September 16, 2011). Those surveyed October 14, 2011–November 4, 2011 were 94% more likely—and those surveyed after November 4, 2011, were 51% more likely—to believe that Mexico is concerned about its immigrants than those surveyed before September 16, 2011. These results suggest that knowing about SP increased immigrants' belief that Mexico cared for its immigrants abroad in a statistically significant way.

Table 2.3 Summary of Ordinal Regression Analysis for Variables Predicting Immigrant's Belief that the Mexican Government Is Concerned about Its Migrants in the US, by Program Promotion Phases in Seguro Popular Project in New York ($N = 849^a$)

	Estimate Coefficients	SE	Wald	DF	P [sig.]	Odds Ratio
List Demographic Variables						
Sex *(women = 1; men = 0)*	−0.046	0.127	0.128	1	0.720	0.96
Age	0.009	0.007	1.706	1	0.192	1.01
Education	0.005	0.019	0.068	1	0.794	1.00
List Immigrant Experience Variables						
Years in the US	−0.003	0.011	0.092	1	0.761	1.00
Undocumented Status *(Undocumented = 1; documented = 0)*[b]	0.193	0.203	0.905	1	0.341	1.21
Having Ever Visited Mexico *(Yes = 1; No = 0)*	0.019	0.158	0.014	1	0.907	1.02
List Intervention Variables						
9/16/11–10/14/11 *(Before 9/16/11 =0, as reference group)*	0.623**	0.163	14.689	1	0.000	1.86
10/14/11–11/04/11 *(Before 9/16/11 = 0, as reference group)*	0.662***	0.171	15.050	1	0.000	1.94
After 11/04/11 *(Before 9/16/11 = 0, as reference group)*	0.415**	0.205	4.098	1	0.043	1.51
Pseudo R^2 (Nagelkerke) = .031**						

Note: Dependent variable *"Mexico is concerned about the welfare of its migrants in the US"* is a 5-point Likert scale. 1 = strongly disagree, 2 = disagree, 3 = indifferent, 4 = agree, 5 = strongly agree.

a   Total number of respondents in the Seguro Popular Survey; significance levels indicated as follows: * $p < 0.05$; **$p < 0.01$; ***$p < 0.001$.

b   Undocumented status predictor is coded as 1 for undocumented and 0 for documented. Undocumented status includes those who reported they were undocumented, who said they had an expired visa, who did not want to answer, and whom the interviewer did not ask about their legal status. Reasons for this coding are explained in the text. Documented status includes those who are US citizens, visa holders, and permanent residents.

Issues Raised by Problems with SP and by Immigrant Leaders

We interviewed and sought to help 39 cases where an immigrant family member had an issue with SP or wanted more information. We took notes and followed up with families after consulting with consular or

SP personnel. We interviewed Mexican community leaders about their knowledge of SP and use of the program, especially organizations helping with access to health care. The following issues arose in our research, which we explore further in Chapters 3 and 4.

Surprise, Happiness, and Incredulity

As detailed above, most immigrants knew nothing about SP. Many didn't believe that it actually existed, or refused to believe that it would cover them. Many who had migrated years earlier said things such as, "They don't worry about us in Mexico. That's why we're *here*! All that corruption. They only want our money." This theme was repeated many times. People told us, "Those in power in Mexico keep everything for themselves, and this corruption made it necessary for us to migrate to the US. Why would we believe they're doing something for us now? What's the political gain for the government?" Contrary to expectations, more respondents believed that Mexico worried about its immigrants. This was especially true for younger immigrants whose families had had positive experiences in Mexico, such as Humberto, whose child's birth was paid for by SP, relieving him of the crippling medical bills he would have incurred at a private clinic. Some immigrants said that their whole families were enrolled, freeing up money they would have spent on medical care for other uses, such as school or better food. In other cases, immigrants weren't aware of SP but believed that the program existed and asked for information to give to their relatives in Mexico to encourage their enrollment in SP.

Complicated Experiences with SP

People with concrete experience of SP often reported complications. We recorded 39 cases where respondents had ill relatives in Mexico. Most greatly appreciated being able to refer their relatives to SP. In six of our 39 cases where someone was ill, the immigrant's family perceived a problem with SP. In one case, an immigrant's father was ill and had been unable to locate an "SP clinic" in or near his hometown. In another case, an immigrant's wife was sick and couldn't figure out how to register for SP, and related that the employees of SP didn't help her do so. Four other cases were more complicated. In one, the immigrant's entire family in Mexico was enrolled in SP, but the local hospital they visited didn't have the medicines they needed and had no specialists, so they had to pay privately for medicine and other doctors. In a second case, the family had SP when the mother became hospitalized. But the Hospital de la Mujer said that SP wouldn't cover the treatment she needed, so they paid out of pocket. Another immigrant's wife was enrolled in SP and became sick, but the hospital refused to pay for tests, referring her to a private, expensive, self-pay hospital. A fourth case involved an immigrant's wife who was enrolled in SP, but the "SP clinic" never kept the appointments she made and sent her to a private clinic instead. These accounts reflect a system that still has glitches and deals with a population unused to making demands in institutional settings, which resonates with Laurell's (2014) critiques.

The response from SP staff with whom we discussed these cases was interesting. One official said these cases were proof that we needed an SP initiative in the US: if immigrants in the US had wider knowledge of SP, they could help their relatives in Mexico by, e.g., helping them find a nearby clinic, hospital, or health center offering SP. The official asked us to imagine how the family member who reported that SP administrators wouldn't help him register could learn *from the immigrant family member* that he has a right to do so and could find out where to go, or at least enlist local municipal authorities to help. While this positive scenario could occur, it would require the immigrant family to act as empowered consumers of health care and for SP and other authorities to respond to them as such.

This explanation also stressed that migrants had authority as heads of household and were more used to making demands because they had lived in the US. We imagined that this theory would become strained when considering more complicated cases, e.g., the clinics and hospitals refusing to treat the family member for free, as SP requires. How would the immigrant in the US (or family member in Mexico) know if the condition was not covered under SP, or whether the doctor or clinic didn't *want* to treat the SP patient, after all? As one hypothetical scenario, perhaps the doctor or clinic would be paid less for treating the patient. We agreed that it would be empowering if the immigrant family member would tell Mexico-residing family members that they have a right to insist on treatment, or to get the generic drug equivalent that's covered by SP. But this scenario presumes that the immigrants would *know* these things about SP, in addition to knowing something about the organization of the program.[8]

Political Motivations, Misperceptions about Health Care, and Reverse Moral Hazards

Three stories about SP dominated our conversations with immigrant leaders: that politics was a motivator for the program; that SP was being misperceived by immigrants and misled them if they had health care decisions to make; and that the program could encourage reckless risk-taking. Immigrant leaders' interpretations were strongly affected by the unequal knowledge that they had of SP and the NY health care system.

Many immigrant leaders saw political motivations at work, holding a general cynicism about the Mexican government's true intentions with SP. Some said SP wasn't new but, rather, old programs combined and being advertised as new. When asked why the government would do that, one leader responded matter-of-factly: an election is coming. Mexico wants to convince immigrants that the government is for them, in order to get votes. Other leaders echoed beliefs about this political motive in promoting SP in an election year.

Several community leaders saw a large, real risk in immigrants' perceptions of SP. To understand their viewpoint, one must consider: (1) the institutional health care decision-making framework facing immigrants and (2) immigrants' perception of SP. What leaders told us, and our surveys bore out, was that most immigrants knew nothing about SP and that many who learned about it were skeptical of the program—not believing that the Mexican government would offer immigrants such a deal. What immigrants believed and what SP covered became critical when local leaders encountered immigrants facing critical health care decisions. In particular, immigrants would hear that the program provided "universal coverage" (*cobertura universal*) and was "a social right" (*un derecho social*), and understand these to mean that Mexicans were being offered health insurance in the US by the Mexican government, or that Mexican immigrants returning to Mexico would be universally covered. They often believed that if they returned to Mexico, their health care needs would be completely met by SP.

One leader relayed conversations with an immigrant with a chronic, serious illness, requiring ongoing care for the rest of his life. The immigrant wanted to return home on the belief that SP would cover all his medical expenses. The leader, however, investigated and couldn't confirm that SP would cover his condition or would cover it completely. So, a first issue was the uncertainty of what SP actually covered. Second, community leaders in NY have become quite knowledgeable about NYC's extensive medical safety net, while knowing much less about SP. These two obstacles would need to be addressed in any larger-scale promotion of SP among Mexicans in the US.

Community leaders pointed out that NYC offered good access to care, even for the poor and undocumented. Child Health Plus offers free health care to everyone under age 21 whose family falls under an income cap. Moreover, NYC's HHC hospitals and a network of other public service hospitals offer comprehensive care on a sliding-scale fee system, which includes those who age out of, or are over age 21 and ineligible for, Child Health or other programs (Rubin, 2009). Immigrant leaders have become knowledgeable about this medical safety net, which, they believe: (1) is much more comprehensive than what's offered by SP; (2) involves less risk of coverage (i.e., it's easy to know for certain if one is covered, as distinct from the ambiguity surrounding what SP covers, especially for migrants); and (3) has few hidden financial liabilities, which they perceived to be a problem with SP. One leader told us, "If we don't know what's covered (in SP), and we don't believe that it will be covered—and we know that health care will be covered for nearly free here—why would we send them back to Mexico?" Leaders worried that seriously ill immigrants would learn about SP on their own and decide to return to Mexico on a mistaken belief that everything is covered.

Leaders outlined a sort of "reverse moral hazard" for SP (Finkelstein et al., 2015). Moral hazards occur when a regulating institution, such as the government, establishes conditions where investors are encouraged to take higher risks because they know the government will cover their losses, as happened in 2008 with the US banking system (Okamoto, 2009–2010). The government's actions can encourage this recklessness, hence the moral hazard. In immigrant leaders' views, if SP promotes universal coverage and contributes to the misunderstanding among immigrants of coverage for everyone, for everything, it will encourage sick immigrants to return to Mexico when ultimately, they would have gotten better care by staying in the US. That is, the Mexican government's actions could encourage immigrants to act against their interests and health because of mistaken beliefs about the generosity or availability of health care in Mexico. The reverse moral hazard occurs because immigrants take the government at face value: they believe they will be covered because this is seen as truly universal coverage, and they act in ways that harm themselves, when staying in NY would have been better.

We've encountered this dilemma of seeking treatment here or returning to use SP in our research for a variety of conditions diagnosed in the US, including a child's autism; a patient with leukemia; and several people with diabetes, heart disease, or related chronic illnesses. In each case, families tried to establish the extent to which these conditions would be covered and how fully, but weren't able to do so before returning to Mexico. Yet a primary positive effect can be for SP to be a subsidy, enabling the family to spend money on something else that they might have had to spend on—e.g., medicine, which is now covered by SP.

This phased research and ongoing discussions with immigrant leaders and immigrants themselves were a foundation for the biggest question emerging from our project (addressed at length in Chapter 3): how should governments, bureaucracies, and other similar institutions communicate with immigrants?

Notes

1 The Hawthorne effect is a widely known dynamic by which the presence of the researcher is believed to affect the outcome of the study. While widely accepted, few studies have data to assess such an effect (Jones, 1992; Smith, 2019; Spano, 2006).

2 The Health Window Program was developed by the Mexican Secretary of Health and the Secretary of Foreign Affairs in 2001, and operates through the Mexican Consulates in the US (http://ventanillas.org).

3 The NY/NJ–based organizations that worked with us on these efforts included: Mano a Mano, the Mexican Consulate, La Unión, Qualitas of Life, Lazos América Unida de New Brunswick, Periódico Nosotros, and Masa.

4 These estimates are based on the huge undercounts of Mexicans in the 1990 and 2000 census, when the population was often newly arrived and had more immigrant than US-citizen persons of Mexican descent, and lived in irregular housing, which wouldn't show up on lists that the census uses to compile its master list of persons. The rate of undercount likely has decreased since 2000, as the Mexican population has become more settled and has about the same number of immigrant and US-citizen persons of Mexican descent. The numbers in 2010 could have been as low as 375,000–400,000 persons. We draw here on Dominguez & Mahler, 1993; de la Puente, 1993; Smith, 1995. In an ongoing study, MIDA's (Mexican Initiative on Deferred Action) research arm found that across NY State, over 97% of Mexican families prescreened for Deferred Action by MIDA lived in overcrowded conditions. For other recent estimates of Mexicans in NYC, see Yrizar Barbosa (2018).

5 The sample we've generated is consistent with previous work on the Mexican population in NY. Backing for this project is provided from a 2011–2012 survey (*n* = 849) and a 2006 CUNY educational survey (*n* = 450), a study of 2002 Mexican Health survey (*n* = 561), and a 1993 study (*n* = 529) of Mexican immigration to NY by Valdes de Montano and Smith (1994). Despite being in different periods, the surveys were conducted in nearly identical fashion, with a large portion of surveys completed in the consulate waiting room, as well as coverage outside the consulate, including public spaces such as Red Hook and Dykeman park soccer fields and churches. These surveys focused on all adults willing to participate. The 1992 and 2006 surveys were mainly completed in the consulate waiting room; the 2006 survey focused on youth who could be college-age, from late teens to late twenties, and almost entirely comprised recently arrived Mexican immigrants. The 1992 survey was a general survey, aimed at getting a profile of the Mexican community. Three of the surveys point to the small diminution of the percentage of immigrants coming from Puebla over 20 years, from 47% in 1992 and 2006, to 42% in 2012, with a slight increase in the

numbers from Oaxaca and Guerrero, the DF (Mexico City), and Estado de México. The 55% from Puebla number in the 2002 survey probably reflects that this was a health-oriented survey and got more women with children—more of whom would likely come from Puebla, with its longer-term settlement than other states. There is a small change in percentage of migration from Oaxaca and Guerrero together, from 18% in 1993 to 15% in 2002, to 18% in 2006 and up to 21% in 2011–2012, probably reflecting an actual increase in migration from those regions. Similarly, there was an increase in the percentage of migration from the DF and Estado de México together, from 11% in 1993 to 12% in 2002, to 14.2% in 2002. The 25% number of those surveyed in the 2006 survey probably reflects its orientation toward education. The relatively higher level of education of those from the DF and Estado de México would have interested them more in the CUNY survey, and led to higher participation rates. These two sites were newer migrant origins than those of Puebla, Oaxaca, and Guerrero, and hence had younger, single people versus family migrants from the Mixteca regions of Puebla, Oaxaca, and Guerrero.

6 The underreporting of undocumented status might be higher because of how we conducted the survey. Given that our goal was to quickly survey a large number of persons and that some hesitated to answer questions about legal status or health care, we tread cautiously. Our policy was not to ask about legal status if the person seemed unduly uncomfortable when asked about status, or when discussing sensitive issues. If we asked about legal status and the person hesitated in answering, we didn't press further, but marked the survey as probably undocumented. The sample had 8.6% preferring not to answer and 12.6% who weren't asked.

7 We also evaluate effects by the dates of our interventions, listed as dummy variables. We coded before and after September 16, 2011, as one dummy variable; another dummy variable was September 17, 2011–October 14, 2011; a third was October 15, 2011–November 4, 2011; and the final one was after November 4, 2011. Those surveyed before September 16, 2011, were the reference group for our two dummy variables.

8 It would be important for immigrants to know that SP doesn't have its own clinics but, rather, offers its services through the State Health Services (SESA) and finances these interventions via CAUSES (Catálogo Universal de Servicios de Salud). Coverage also exists through the Fondo de Protección Contra Gastos Catastróficos y el Seguro Médico para una Nueva Generación.

3   How Should We Communicate with Immigrants?

Following from the research in the first part of this book, which revealed immigrants' lack of knowledge about and misperceptions of Seguro Popular (SP), we conducted further research to discover which communication and social marketing strategies could best meet these challenges.[1] Immigrants didn't know about SP, or understood it to be a free government program offering universal coverage for all illnesses and conditions to all Mexicans, rather than the more limited yet still important government program it is. Indeed, *some 73% of the more than 800 persons we surveyed had no knowledge of SP* (aside from what they had learned from the surveyor), and the longer that one had lived in the US, the lower the chances the individual knew about SP.

Given that SP has given many more Mexicans and all children born after 2005 access to some type of health care, where most hadn't had it before, we observed astounding disconnects between the Mexican government's intended messages and what Mexicans in NY actually understood. Immigrants and community leaders had low levels of concrete knowledge about SP, and thus were unsure of whether to use it. As a result of these misperceptions and uncertainties, immigrant community leaders were reluctant or even skeptical to recommend this program to immigrants in NY. They had a variety of theories about SP's purpose and its utility for those with whom they worked. We sought to understand how governments and similar institutions should communicate with immigrants, following calls in the literature to continue developing culturally relevant campaigns and materials in health care with immigrant populations (Asgedom, 2015; Karan, 2008; Lovejoy & Saxton, 2012; Magro, 2012; Sabogal & Cordingley-Klein, 1999; Sugarman et al., 2011; Williams & Kumanyika, 2003).

Social Marketing Approaches for Local and Transnational Communication

In the second part of this book, we forward a social marketing approach to communicating with transnational audiences. Above other considerations, marketing for public causes should primarily focus on asking target audiences to engage in one or a few key *behaviors* (Lee & Kotler, 2016). Social marketers always go beyond simple awareness or education efforts, instead asking audiences to *do* something as the result of a communication campaign: call a particular phone number, fill out personal information on a website, or visit a certain place, among other options. Social marketing and related fields are unanimous on this point (see also Andresen, 2006; for an overview of the many problems of "awareness" and "education" campaigns, see Christiano & Neimand, 2017; Singal, 2014). A behavior isn't necessarily the specific message for a campaign; instead, it provides a clear purpose and helps shape messaging in a measurable way: did individuals carry out the intended behavior? At a minimum, did the behavior increase or decrease? Asking audiences to take particular actions as a result of messages already incorporates "awareness" within its design: when asking audiences to take an action, they already must understand what a program or initiative is about. Categories of behavior like "safer sex" or "healthy eating" aren't what we're after (Hornik, 2013) but specific, measurable actions such as "sign this online commitment form" or "eat one fruit or vegetable every day at lunch." Any calls for actionable information in the second half of this book follow from getting audiences to engage in certain behaviors.

Social marketing approaches are keenly attentive to *barriers*, or perceived audience objections to communication and outreach, such as confusion about what a program offers or a belief that visiting a clinic may take too long or be too far away. These objections are critical in forming new strategies for better communication about public programs. In addition to reviewing connected literature and examining existing materials, researchers using a social marketing approach should conduct research on what target audiences think about programs, messages, and more. Through methods like "concept testing," social marketers contrast the typical

> "expert-driven" decisions of what behavior people "should" engage in and the theoretical hypotheses of "why" they are (or are not) motivated to do so against the realities of the priority group we seek to serve. Concept testing focuses social marketers on being

close to people, audience-driven versus maintaining an expert role in which decisions are made and carried out without considering the [point of view] and voice of people.

(Lefebvre, 2015, para. 2)

Historically, large organizations such as government agencies thought that self-evident arguments or well-designed messages created by experts were all that was needed to communicate with their publics (Dervin & Foreman-Wernet, 2013, pp. 150–151). The original proponents of public campaigns never imagined a time when informational expertise would be challenged, or when governments or other bureaucracies could be perceived as abusive or misleading in their research, so it's critical to create campaigns in which "institutions hear more than they speak" (p. 148). Organizations should consider the populations they serve as "participants in a democracy" rather than simply "consumers of information" (Dorfman & Wallack, 2013, p. 339).

We employed this social marketing approach in our research on the use of SP by Mexicans in NY. We conducted interviews and focus groups with relevant stakeholders to gain a deeper sense of how immigrants understood SP. Our point of departure for the second round of research was the insight from SegPop1 that SP needed to be far clearer about what it actually *is* so that it wouldn't be rejected by Mexicans in NY for what it's not. After presenting our findings below, we offer recommendations that combine tested research, social marketing theory, and strategies in public communication that can be transferred to immigration, health care, and similar campaigns. These include Internet, social media, and other strategies (Aaker & Smith, 2010). We offer these lessons from the SP project, but the approach is easily adaptable for other campaigns by the US or Mexican governments, as well as nonprofits or other institutions around the world.

Research Strategy

Focus groups and interviews enable researchers to access how informants think about issues. Interviews provide insight into a single person's thinking; focus groups provide a social context in which informants give opinions about their experiences. Focus groups enable researchers to see informants in social interaction and observe how one informant's perception or belief is mirrored, muted, or negated by others' responses. Focus groups also enable researchers to observe how a current of opinion gets picked up (or not) by other members of the group (Smith, 2006; Wilkinson, 1998). Good campaigns don't just assume that audiences need the information we have for them; rather, they "use formative research such as focus groups to develop messages and inform campaign strategy" and link results with community programs and policy advocacy to provide structural support for changes (Dorfman & Wallack, 2013, p. 336). Focus groups allow the testing of various media such as video, websites and related images, comics, and approach scripts for introducing or disseminating information with potential participants.

Focus Groups with Interactive Materials and Two Phases

Our first round of focus groups focused on participants' impressions of SP and materials about SP. The first focus-group guide asked about the group's knowledge and understanding of SP, including what the informants thought the program *was* and what the program *was not*, and the positive or negative experiences they or their acquaintances had had with it. Section I of our guide showed two videos of immigrants in NY (explained in more detail below). Section II included a summary about SP, and asked about group dispositions to recommend SP to friends and family—and what information participants thought would induce them to use SP (or, for community or organization leaders, to recommend their clients use it). In Section III, we showed three kinds of media about SP: a video by the government (Secretary of Health) on YouTube; the SP Internet page; and the SP pamphlet or comic book that the Mexican Consulate in NY distributed.[2] We recorded participants' reactions and assessments of these instruments. Section IV asked informants if they were likely, after viewing these materials, to encourage their family and friends to use SP and, if not, why. We asked what information they would need to recommend it to others. We asked informants how the program should be promoted, including specific language it should include and if legal status makes a difference in people's desire to use it. Section V asked where informants received trusted information about health care decisions, what types of incentives or knowledge would make them or their families use SP, what places would be most convenient to use SP, and what kinds of media could best communicate information about SP to people like them.[3]

In a second round of focus groups, we sought information that would enable us to make recommendations to SP about how to talk with the immigrant population in NY and their families in Mexico. Section I of our guide showed two videos—of Humberto and Mayra, who had knowledge of SP during SegPop1. As mentioned, Humberto is a young man whose wife in Mexico just had a baby and received medical care from SP; he pronounced the program *demasiado bueno* ("too good"). Mayra is an immigrant who felt happier knowing that her relatives and other immigrants' relatives could be healthier in Mexico using SP's benefits. Using common social marketing techniques, we asked the informants what they thought Humberto and Mayra were saying (and what they would have liked them to say) and what these short videos were aimed at getting them to do.

In these second focus groups, we asked about immigrants' use of the media, including TV, radio, newspapers, and Internet on weekdays and weekends. We tested four scripts for presenting SP to immigrants (reproduced below). We prepared each text using our previous interviews and other research; each intends to appeal to a different *identity* held by immigrants. The broadest identity was immigrants who might return to Mexico, which theoretically includes all Mexican immigrants in NY (represented in the Venn diagrams in Figure 3.1) as the largest circle, inside which all the other identities are nested.

We initially posited that the identities of *jefes/jefas de familia* ("male/ female heads of households"), and *hijos/hijas ausentes* ("absent sons/ daughters") or *nietos/nietas* of *abuelitos/abuelitas* ("grandsons/grand-daughters" of "grandfathers/grandmothers") would also appeal. Identities that people connect to and take pride in are especially important motivators for people to change their behavior (Heath & Heath, 2010). Empirical campaign research recognizes that health promotion messages focused on modeling positive, attainable identities—rather than stigmatizing, "fear-based messages about disease and risk behaviors"—are superior motivational strategies for achieving health outcomes (Colarossi et al., 2016, p. 1). We speculated that the identity of Mexicans who may return to Mexico because of a serious or chronic illness might be a more limited but compelling identity for action, so it is included as the smallest part of the diagram below.

Why be so specific about these identities? Dillard, Weber, and Vail (2007) found in a meta-analysis that pretesting messages helps predict message effectiveness (cited in Atkin & Freimuth, 2013). New ideas can arise in audience responses, particularly the generation of words, phrases, and vernacular that motivate audiences. For example, the National Cancer Institute found that for many people, the word "risk" raises alarm, while "chance" minimizes it, when speaking about cancer (Atkin & Freimuth, 2013, p. 61). Even vague or unfamiliar terms such as "fourfold" can give people reason to discount information (pp. 61–62).[4] According to the US Department of Health and Human Services, a test of a booklet on lung cancer showed that patients remembered only two out of 12 ideas presented, on average, while half couldn't remember any because of too much jargon, concepts that the audience deemed irrelevant, or a lack of distinction between diagnostic and treatment procedures that inhibited audience recall of the information (p. 63). Health campaigns must therefore consider each framing and word choice strategically to reach audiences. The complexity of conducting a health care campaign across borders only amplifies this need.

In Figure 3.1, diagram A, the category of people with low income, *escasos recursos* ("scarce resources"), cuts across the other categories/ identities, including *jefes/jefas de familia, hijos/hijas*, and people who might return or who have a serious illness. In diagram B, we used the category of low income not as an identity but as a broader circle that includes the other audiences. The difference between diagrams A and B is that the former refers to immigrant identities that are independent of each other, while the latter is framed in terms of audiences and a "hierarchy of identities" as the focus for a public policy.

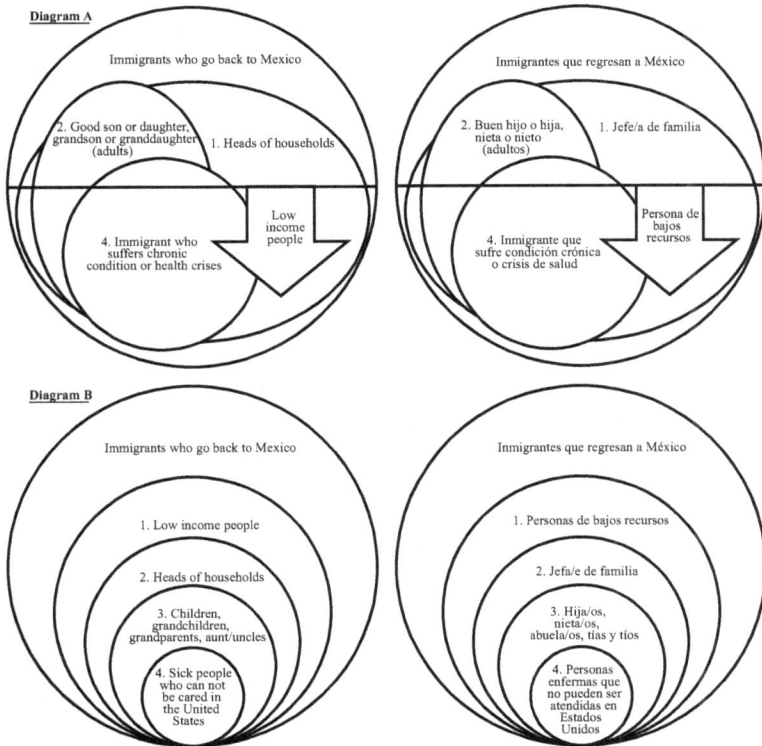

Figure 3.1 Four Target Groups for SP and Mexicans in New York.

We tested identities often used in outreach literature by the Mexican government—e.g., in its Programa Paisano or literature from the IME (Instituto de los Mexicanos en el Exterior). These identities included those of *migrante* and *paisano* ("countryman"). We included the identity of a person with *escasos recursos* because it was raised repeatedly by informants in our research. These identities were used in a combined way in the scripts below.[5] We asked about concepts often invoked in the scholarly literature on transnational life, including *hijos/ hijas ausentes* in scripts 1 and 2.

Script 1:

¡Migrantes mexicanos! ¡Jefas y jefes de familia! ¡Ahora puedes estar presente aunque estés ausente! Cuida la salud de tus seres queridos y diles que se inscriban al Seguro Popular, que es un seguro médico limitado para personas de bajos recursos que viven en México y que no tienen acceso al IMSS o el ISSSTE. ¡Es gratis y de bajo costo! Puedes atender desde un embarazo hasta ciertos tipos de cáncer. ¡Migrante! Tú puedes cumplir con tus responsabilidades como madre y padre al decirle a tu familia que se inscriba al Seguro Popular. También puedes protegerte al pre-afiliarte en el consulado más cercano, para que cuando vuelvas también tengas atención médica.

Script 1:

Mexican migrants! Female and male heads of family! Now you can be present even if you are absent. Care about your loved ones' health by telling them to enroll in Seguro Popular, a limited medical-insurance program for low-income people living in Mexico who don't have access to IMSS or ISSSTE. It's free and low-cost! You can receive care from a pregnancy up to certain types of cancer. Migrant! You can fulfill your responsibilities as a mother and father when you tell your family to enroll in Seguro Popular. You can also protect yourself when you pre-enroll at the nearest consulate, so that when you return, you can also have medical care.

Script 2:

¡Paisano! ¡Paisana! Ahora puedes cuidar la salud de tu familia aunque estés fuera de México. Los hijos, hijas, nietas y nietos ausentes pueden proteger a sus papás y abuelitos al invitarlos a que se inscriban al Seguro Popular. Todas las personas de bajos recursos en México que no tienen otro seguro pueden afiliarse pues son

"elegibles." También puedes proteger tu salud al pre-afiliarte en el consulado más cercano, para que cuando vuelvas también tengas atención médica.

Script 2:

Countryman! Countrywoman! Now you can take care of your family's health while you are away from Mexico. Absent sons, daughters, grandsons, and granddaughters can protect their parents and grandparents by inviting them to enroll in Seguro Popular. All low-income people in Mexico without any other insurance can enroll because they're eligible. You can also protect your health when you pre-enroll at the nearest consulate, so that when you return, you can also have medical care.

Script 3:

¡Paisano! Aprovecha tu próximo viaje a México para que vayas a ver al doctor. ¡Que sean unas vacaciones saludables! Pre-afíliate al Seguro Popular en tu consulado más cercano para que cuando vuelvas a México sea más fácil recibir atención médica. Aunque no estés enfermo ahorita, pre-afíliate para que puedes recibir información preventiva, te servirá para mantener tu salud y fuerza. ¡Aprovecha! ¡No vaya a ser la de malas! Los migrantes inteligentes y fuertes son los migrantes que buscan atención médica preventiva cuando están en su país. ¡Usa tu derecho a la salud en México para mantenerte fuerte y saludable!

Script 3:

Countryman! Take advantage of your next trip to Mexico so that you can go to the doctor. Make it a healthy vacation! Pre-enroll in Seguro Popular at your nearest consulate, so that when you return to Mexico, it will be easier to receive medical care. Although you're not sick right now, pre-enroll so that you can receive preventive information; this will help you keep your health and strength. Take advantage! Don't wait for bad news! Intelligent and strong migrants are those seeking preventive medical care when they're in their country. Use your right to health in Mexico to stay strong and healthy!

Script 4:

Migrante, si vuelves a México, pre-afíliate al Seguro Popular para que tengas acceso a la atención médica en tu país. Para averiguar cuáles son tus opciones de atención medica si piensas volver a México, pasa por tu consulado local para consultar a la gente de la Ventanilla de Salud. El Seguro Popular ofrece atención médica a toda persona de bajos recursos en México. Como migrante y persona que necesita ayuda inscríbete al Seguro Popular para que tengas acceso a atención médica gratuita. Sin embargo recuerda que el Seguro Popular es una póliza que ofrece cobertura para muchas condiciones, pero no para todas las enfermedades. Acércate entonces a la Ventanilla de Salud de tu consulado para averiguar tus opciones. Cualquier decisión sobre tu salud o la de tu familia es mejor que sea tomada consultando un médico en tu idioma y tu país.

Script 4:

Migrant, if you return to Mexico, pre-enroll in Seguro Popular so that you can have access to medical attention in your country. To find out what your options are for medical care if you are thinking of returning to Mexico, go to your local consulate to consult with people at the Health Window. Seguro Popular offers medical attention to all low-income people in Mexico. As a migrant and a person who needs help, you can enroll in Seguro Popular so that you can have access to free medical care. However, remember that Seguro Popular is an insurance policy that offers coverage for many conditions but not for all diseases. Go to the Health Window in your consulate to find out about your options. Any decision about your health, or the health of your family, is better made consulting a doctor in your language and your country.

Our focus-group selection was designed to gain access to different, key demographics that could offer insight into how users (or potential users) of SP would respond to materials. We selected groups likely to reflect different kinds of SP users, with different relationships to the consulate and to US institutions and with different levels of settlement in the US.

We began with three focus groups in community organizations with distinct demographics: (1) more recently arrived, undocumented day laborers (only men) who are less established in the US and live more precarious lives in NY, and are associated with a new organization serving their interests (El Centro del Inmigrante on Staten Island); (2) mothers who have been in NY for varying periods—but who have all had children in NY and send them to school in the state—and who participate in an educational organization (Masa in the Bronx) offering after-school services to children (which has collaborated with the Mexican Consulate and NYC Department of Education on projects); and (3) a mixed group of more long-term established men and women affiliated with an advocacy and organizing group (La Unión in Brooklyn) that focuses on mobilization and social rights and has been critical of the NYC Department of Education and Mexican Consulate.

These three focus groups were selected because they allowed access to different demographic types and because our research team had good relationships with leaders of the organizations, who each agreed to serve as hosts for the focus groups (Figures 3.2 and 3.3). We anticipated that the most recently arrived, undocumented immigrants whose lives were more precarious (El Centro) would be most appreciative of SP and any help that could be offered, while those whose politics criticized the Department of Education (La Unión) would be more critical of SP. We speculated that those who had worked more in conjunction with the Department of Education (Masa) would be in between. These expectations were largely borne out.

We completed two other focus groups inside the consulate, one with men and one with women. We did focus groups outside and inside the consulate, as we suspected that doing focus groups in the consulate might dampen criticism or skepticism of SP among participants, or that the political engagement of some focus-group members might heighten such criticism. Below, we report the first three community-organization-based focus groups together, and then move into a second section that discusses the focus groups completed in the consulate.

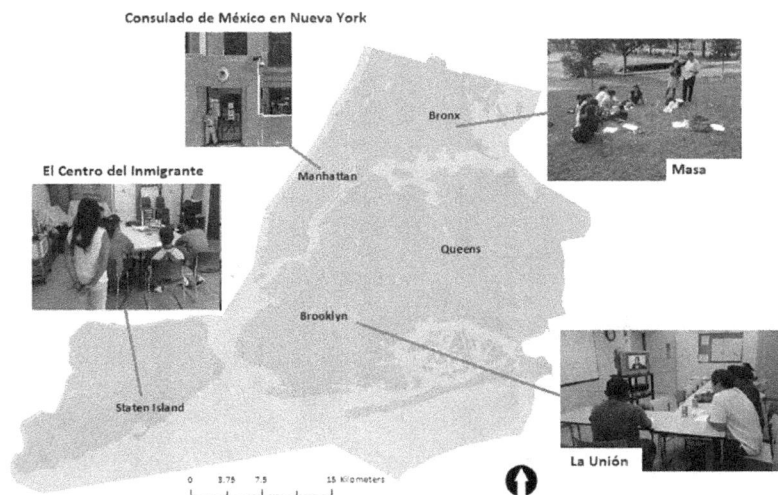

Figure 3.2 Focus Groups in Four NYC Locations: Bronx (Masa), Staten Island (El Centro del Inmigrante), Brooklyn (La Unión), and Manhattan (Consulado General de México).

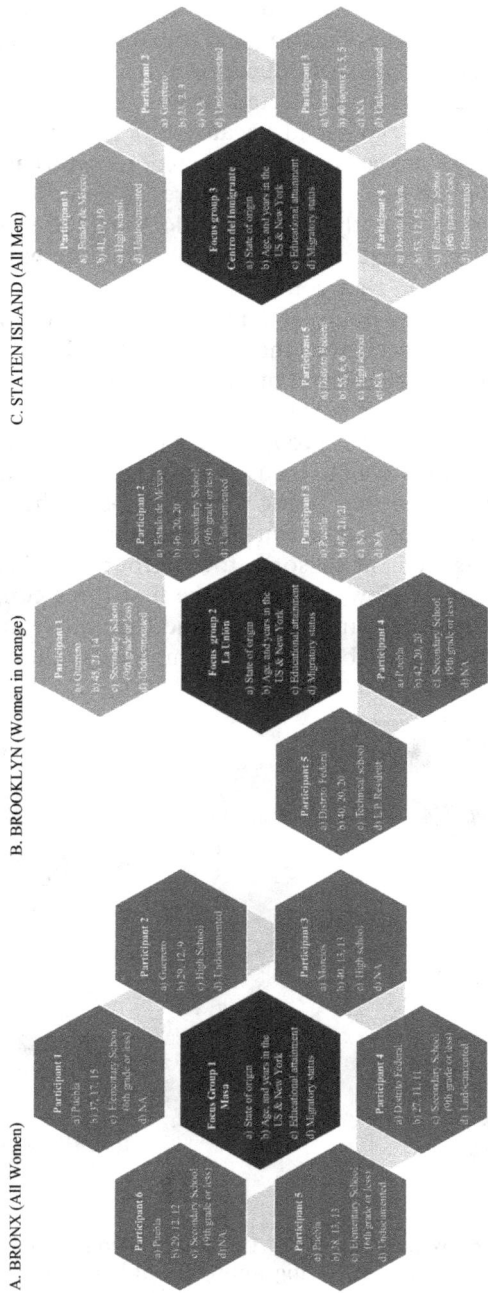

A. BRONX (All Women)

B. BROOKLYN (Women in orange)

C. STATEN ISLAND (All Men)

A. BRONX (All Women)

Participant 1
a) Puebla
b) 37, 12, 15
c) Elementary School (6th grade or less)
d) NA

Participant 2
a) Guerrero
b) 29, 12, 9
c) High School
d) Undocumented

Participant 3
a) Morelos
b) 40, 15, 13
c) High school
d) NA

Focus Group 1
Mesa
a) State of origin
b) Age, and years in the US & New York
c) Educational attainment
d) Migratory status

Participant 4
a) Distrito Federal
b) 27, 11, 11
c) Secondary School (9th grade or less)
d) Undocumented

Participant 5
a) Puebla
b) 15, 13, 13
c) Elementary School (6th grade or less)
d) Undocumented

Participant 6
a) Puebla
b) 29, 12, 12
c) Secondary School (9th grade or less)
d) NA

B. BROOKLYN (Women in orange)

Participant 1
a) Guerrero
b) 68, 39, 14
c) Secondary School (9th grade or less)
d) Undocumented

Participant 2
a) Estado de México
b) 46, 20, 20
c) Secondary School (9th grade or less)
d) Undocumented

Participant 3
a) Puebla
b) 47, 21, 21
c) NA
d) NA

Focus group 2
La Unión
a) State of origin
b) Age, and years in the US & New York
c) Educational attainment
d) Migratory status

Participant 4
a) Puebla
b) 42, 20, 20
c) Secondary School (9th grade or less)
d) NA

Participant 5
a) Distrito Federal
b) 40, 20, 20
c) Technical school
d) LP Resident

C. STATEN ISLAND (All Men)

Participant 1
a) Estado de México
b) 41, 10, 10
c) High school
d) Undocumented

Participant 2
a) Guerrero
b) NA
c) NA
d) Undocumented

Focus group 3
Centro del Inmigrante
a) State of origin
b) Age, and years in the US & New York
c) Educational attainment
d) Migratory status

Participant 3
a) Veracruz
b) 40, between 3, 5, 5
c) NA
d) Undocumented

Participant 4
a) Distrito Federal
b) 53, 12, 12
c) Secondary school (9th grade or less)
d) Undocumented

Participant 5
a) Distrito Federal
b) 55, 1, 6
c) High school
d) NA

Figure 3.3 Basic Demographic Information for the Three Focus Groups outside Manhattan for SegPop2.

Interviews

In addition to our focus groups, we conducted anonymous interviews with several community leaders to discuss their impressions of SP, of how immigrants understood it, and how it might best be disseminated. As with the focus groups, one criterion included selecting informants who varied in their previous stances on criticizing, supporting, or working in or with the Mexican government or the consulate in NY. We expected that those who had previously been the most (or least) critical of the Mexican government or Consulate would be the most (or least) critical of SP. In all cases, we picked community leaders who had at least some experience working with SP or the NY-based health care system, so that we reached a wide range of publics in the field—i.e., leaders who were relatively informed about the various health care options for immigrants.

We realized that we would need to engage debates about policy dissemination. Research on *policy narratives* often discusses the stories that politicians tell to justify a particular policy, or how others who disagree with the policy reframe it by telling a different story (Abbott, 2001; Boyce, 1995; Ewick & Silbey, 1995; Gamson & Modigliani, 1989; Hajer, 1995; Hajer & Laws, 2006; Jacobs & Sobieraj, 2007; Pease Chock, 1995; Somers, 1994; Snow & Benford, 1992). While we initially framed the project using the literature on policy narratives, we switched to a social marketing approach because it offered a broader set of theoretical and empirical tools for applied research—it moved us beyond efforts at dissemination or "awareness" in favor of behavioral, actionable outcomes and the structural and community changes that support them. A policy narrative framework looks at the stories that politicians or institutions tell to legitimize the policy choices they want to make. A social marketing framework takes into account such stories but also looks at the realistic, material factors that could affect these symbolic choices, such as the monetary costs or institutional partnerships that could be involved in promoting collective actions.

Most theories of decision making in health care focus on how individuals make their decisions. Various theories include: a rational decision-making model asserting that patients do a cost-benefit analysis in making health care decisions; models theorizing that patients and often doctors have incomplete information and hence make decisions based partly on assumptions; and models emphasizing that patients "feel" their way through decisions, led by emotions and values (Banning, 2008; Baron, 2004; Ubel, 2010).

Our cases required another set of analytical tools because immigrants' lives are in two countries. Immigrants, especially recent immigrants most likely to have relatives living in Mexico who are eligible for SP, face the normal vagaries of medical decision making but also live in a transnationalized social space with ongoing family relations with those left behind in Mexico. They must make decisions affecting their families, while not present with them. Although their social and family life is transnationalized, they tend to make health-care decisions in places that are decidedly *not* transnational. Policy eligibility for access to health care is most often based on geography, the local medical and community institutional context, legal status, and factors such as knowledge of the programs. Geography affects access because one's access to health care depends on where one lives. Those living in NYC, for example, usually have access to a comprehensive public health care system that covers most conditions, even if one has no legal documentation (Sanders, 2014). Those living in NY State but outside NYC, or living in NJ, have fewer options. One must live in Mexico to receive services through SP. Those with legal status or citizenship in the US often have much better health care access than those without it, although this, too, varies by location.

Using a social marketing perspective, we propose a model of health-care decision making that describes the actual conditions and use of SP and related health care decisions that immigrants make, including their lack of complete information about all options, reliance on friends' advice, and the need to fit their decisions into the rest of their lives. We need to differentiate between those who must make this decision themselves because they're sick, and those who are making this decision while healthy. Healthy persons are less likely to feel urgency in making health care decisions, so we must appeal to other identities and sentiments. Rather than appealing only to sick persons who need health care now for a crisis, we should also appeal to persons who would be caring for their families by getting regular health care, or identifying Mexico as a place that takes care of people when they're home to visit family.

Focus groups and interviews are especially useful in gauging responses to media aimed at promoting knowledge of a product (Wilkinson, 1998). We oriented the section of our focus groups in which we asked informants to respond to ads or scripts around three sets of questions: (1) What's the *main message* of this video?, (2) What is it that they *say*? What do they not say? What would you like them to say? What are your responses?, and (3) What do these ads want you to *do*? The social marketing literature indicates that these are key questions for any outreach campaign seeking to change perceptions and create action around a program (Lee & Kotler, 2016).

Key Findings

First Round of Community-Based Focus Groups

The three community-based focus groups primarily comprised un-documented, Mexican adult immigrants and heads of family, mostly between 35 and 45. They came from Puebla, México, Guerrero, Veracruz, and Morelos and from the DF (now CDMX, or Mexico City). Most had basic, elementary school educations; some had secondary education. Participants had been in NY between 3 and 21 years, with an average of 13 years. This estimate squared with our numbers from the larger sample in SegPop1, where the average age was 36 and average years in the US was 11.7.

As discussed previously and shown in Figure 3.1(A), the focus group in the Bronx, at Masa, comprised women united in their focus on education and participation in an after-school educational program that offered homework help and related services to children. The group in Brooklyn, related to La Unión, was a more activist group and had slightly higher educational levels than the other groups. It comprised men and women. The group at El Centro del Inmigrante in Port Richmond, Staten Island, comprised more recently arrived, undocumented men who are day laborers, and hence were less in-tegrated into US life and institutions. They had the lowest levels of education and the highest levels of marginalization. While members of the Masa and La Unión groups were somewhat wary of what the consulate might offer, the men from El Centro del Inmigrante were enthusiastic about the Consulate on Wheels that had come to their site on Staten Island.

The three groups lacked knowledge of and hesitated to express knowledge about SP. As discussed in SegPop1, most immigrants left for the US before SP was implemented, and certainly before it was well known or commonly used; but more recent arrivals knew more about it. There was confusion about what SP offered and if the program stood alone or was part of a related program—e.g., Oportunidades or IMSS. Brand confusion emerged among focus-group members, who couldn't clearly differentiate between these programs.

Respondents in the focus groups said they didn't have enough in-formation about SP to have a clear sense of what the program offered from the materials we showed them. They noted that the pamphlet that the consulate distributes didn't have a local phone number that potential users could call to get more information if they were in the US. The lack of a telephone number or other such information violated an imperative in the social marketing approach—that one give people actionable information and ask them to do something.

For the promotional clip from SP that we showed, participants appreciated being told that SP existed and could be helpful, but they wanted more actionable information. In each group, participants reiterated that they wanted promotional materials to offer certain services: *que digan exactamente lo que sí ofrecen y lo que no* ("they should say exactly what they offer and what they do not"), *que digan dónde se ofrece* ("they should say where it's offered"), and *que digan a quien sí cubre y a quien no* ("they should say who it covers and who it does not"). The three groups focused on how SP promotional materials mentioned that the program was for people *de escasos recursos económicos* ("economically disadvantaged") and that they identified with this group.

The three groups noted that the publicity materials from SP were designed to promote awareness of the program. But they thought that these materials didn't offer sufficient information about the kinds of illnesses that might be covered. They wanted more actionable information that they could understand and use to orient their behavior (Hibbard, 2003). SP wanted to disseminate information useful to the whole population, but the focus groups revealed that immigrants wanted information to use in their particular cases. We acknowledge that no dissemination program can address all the great variety of illnesses that can occur in a population, but it should pitch its efforts to a range of audiences and identities. As social marketers frequently state, "one size never fits all" when it comes to communicating with large audiences (Lee & Kotler, 2011, p. 129).

There was great interest in knowing more about SP to become beneficiaries and to promote its use among family members and friends in Mexico. The main problems were that our focus-group participants didn't know what SP offered, who could participate, and what level of detail might be sufficient to make that information actionable. In all three focus groups, participants suggested using social media and related technologies in outreach. All the groups discussed Facebook (FB) as one source for doing so. Members of each group used FB to keep in touch with family in Mexico and elsewhere in the US, or had their children do it for them. They used the text-chat functions and liked to share photos on FB. They mentioned embedding links into one's FB page as a potentially useful way to promote information about SP. Participants mentioned text messages to their cell phones as another useful way to disseminate information, as they had been receptive to sales solicitations to their cell phones.

Second Round of Community-Based Focus Groups

The second round of community-based focus groups drew on insights from the first round, from the report for SegPop1, and from literature and our team's meetings. As discussed, we first showed the respondents two videos we made from SegPop1, of Humberto and Mayra, and asked what the videos were trying to convey and what they wanted viewers to do. We then asked them about their own use of media and to respond to several scripts we had developed for possible communication about SP.

Reactions to Humberto's video were positive, but participants wanted more information. From Humberto's video, and the text that preceded and followed his testimonial, participants understood that: (1) SP was for anyone of any socioeconomic level, (2) one can pre-enroll, and (3) SP was promoting a health-insurance policy. From Humberto's testimonial, members of El Centro del Inmigrante focus group understood him to be saying that his wife had had a baby with the help of SP, that one should ensure that his/her family is covered, and that SP is trustworthy. But they noted that he didn't say what ages were covered, how to pre-enroll or where, or anything about the particulars of what was covered and how much it cost.

The La Unión focus group understood Humberto to say that his wife had had a baby, that she had been well attended to, and it hadn't cost them a lot of money. This group also understood SP as a product, an insurance policy, that they could buy. But participants didn't get such information as cost: *¡Se necesita saber el costo!* ("You need to know the cost!"), said one member. Participants remarked that they wanted more actionable information, e.g., the phone number of the consulate or elsewhere to call for more information. From Humberto's video, Masa's focus-group participants understood SP to be an insurance policy with 100% full coverage for all medical costs, or low medical costs. They understood that Humberto's wife had had a positive experience with her pregnancy and that SP could grant anyone an opportunity to have coverage.

Reactions to Mayra's video were slightly different, partly because of the different emphasis in the two stories. While Humberto focused on his own family's experience with having a baby whose birth expenses were covered by SP, Mayra urged others to make use of SP to protect their families. Mayra was enthusiastic and smiling, while some thought that Humberto looked a little nervous. Participants in El Centro del Inmigrante remarked that Mayra looked as though *ella se siente más segura* ("she feels safer"), and *ella está contenta porque su familia está segura con respecto al a salud* ("she's happy that her family is safe with respect to health"). Participants in La Unión noted that Mayra didn't say whether she was enrolled and that she never gave details and actionable information. They recommended making *un comercial profesional* (a professional commercial). But they recommended *un comercial sincero* (an authentic commercial) with "real" people like Humberto and Mayra and trustworthy characters like a nurse or doctor. Masa participants commented on Mayra's happiness and sense of security in knowing that her family was covered; however, they were quick to note that, although she had had a good experience, they had to try it and have the same experience to believe it. Two out of the three participants had close friends or family members who hadn't had such a positive experience and thus were skeptical of the video. They saw the video as "pure politics" and compared it to Mexican presidents who don't honor their word.

The differences between the three community-based focus groups may represent differences in how each interacted with US and Mexican society. Members of La Unión have a social-justice agenda and consider themselves immigrants from the "global south." Participants from Masa were engaged with an after-school program that worked more closely with the educational system, challenging it less directly and having a less politicized perspective. Even those with relatively fewer years in the US saw themselves as being in NY for the long term and had many relatives still in Mexico. Many reported that their families had had negative experiences with SP in Mexico, and especially that their expectations about what SP would cover weren't met. The people from El Centro del Inmigrante were more recently arrived in the US and had more immediate needs for simple survival. Among the groups, they were most positive about the Consulate on Wheels and the support they got from El Centro—and the least critical of SP.

Reactions to the Four Scripts

The four scripts we prepared were designed to elicit responses from the informants and determine what identities they would react to most positively or negatively. We crafted the scripts, presented above, in response to findings from SegPop1 and to our first round of focus groups. We drew from the language of long-term campaigns and styles of outreach used by the Mexican government in its Paisano programs and in its initiatives for IME and SRE, including the identities of *migrante*, *paisano*, and *jefe/jefa de familia*.

Focus-group participants supported script 4 the most and script 1 the least, while the others had more mixed support. They uniformly did not endorse the appeal to *jefe/jefa de familia, ama de casa* ("housewife"), *migrante Mexicano* ("Mexican migrant"), *amigo migrante* ("migrant friend"), or *migrante*. Participants at the second focus group in Brooklyn and Staten Island said, *se oye feo* ("it sounds ugly") to the last identity—as they associated the term with the police or US border-patrol agents. For many Mexican immigrants in the US, it is mainly US customs and border-patrol agents who refer to them as *migrante*. The term *migrante* also reminded them of, in the words of one participant in Brooklyn, *la tragedia y dolor de la separación de las familias* ("the tragedy and pain of families' separations").

Ethnographic fieldwork and interviews with Mexican immigrants from different states of origin, living in Mexico or in the US, indicate that the Spanish terms *la migración, la inmigración, el emigrante*, or just *la migra* are commonly used to refer to US immigration authorities in their everyday communication (Alarcón & Yrizar Barbosa, 2015). Similarly, *familia migrante* wasn't popular. One participant didn't like being referred to in the script as *migrante Mexicano* because such an appellation was used to *nos ponen en un lugar* ("put us in our place"). It was a reminder that they were immigrants, while those drafting the message were more privileged members of the government. They especially disliked the idea that consular personnel would give them materials addressing them this way, or address them this way themselves, because it highlighted social differences. While migrants came to the US out of economic need and endured many struggles in NY, they saw consular staff as coming voluntarily and living lives of comparative comfort. There were mixed reactions to *paisano* or *paisa*. The more recently arrived and undocumented workers in El Centro del Inmigrante especially did not support it: they thought that this form of address is usually used between *gente de confianza* ("trustworthy people") and *amigos* ("friends"). Those with more time and who were more settled in La Unión group liked it better. Participants didn't like *hijos/hijas ausentes*, or *ausentes siempre presentes* ("the absent always present") because they didn't understand them—surprising, because both these phrases were generated by immigrant leaders.

Interestingly, participants accepted the identity of *personas de bajos recursos* ("low-income people") because they felt it described themselves in Mexico and in NY. The phrase they supported most was *Mexicanos* or *Mexicanos en Nueva York* ("Mexicans in New York"). Given the reasons for not liking the other identities, we believe that this was seen as the most neutral/positive identity, as it neither reminded participants of the losses that migration had forced on them (e.g., family separation) nor highlighted the status and class differences between themselves and those who were making the appeals to them. Using an identity that immigrants viewed as neutral or positive may help with the catch-22 that the Mexican government and consulates may find themselves in when approaching immigrants abroad. Immigrants, particularly those who have been in the US a long time, may blame the Mexican government for creating the conditions that led them to leave, even while they like and seek connection with the consulate in helping them. These identities and emotions are intensified in the consulate waiting room, where immigrants wait for long periods through a set of highly bureaucratized interactions (Goffman, 1961), with staff that can intensify the feeling that those in the consulate—and, by extension, in the government in Mexico—aren't like the rest of us who came here out of need.

The consulate has made the process of getting documents more responsive and efficient (e.g., by giving approximate appointment times, which wasn't done in the past), so the persistence of this dynamic is ironic. Identities that bypass terms such as "migrant" and emphasize the commonality between immigrants and consular staff (e.g., as *Mexicanos en Nueva York*) make clear that governments should empirically test their outreach materials when communicating with such audiences. Figure 3.4 is a graphic synthesis of the reactions to the identities we posed to participants in the community-based focus groups, where the sphere containing the identity of *personas de bajos recursos* underscores the positive reaction that provoked, and *familia migrante* as an association with a negative label. The identities in the other spheres have been commonly used in US–Mexico migration literature, while others have been used in the dissemination of Mexican

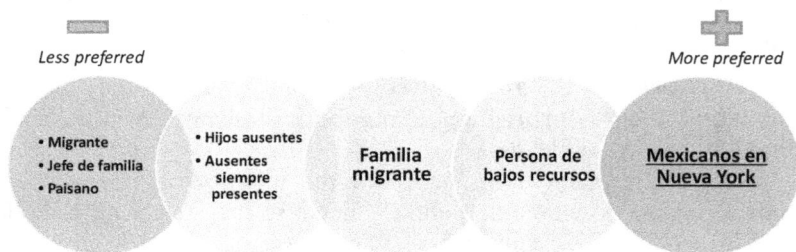

Less preferred   More preferred

- Migrante   • Hijos ausentes   Familia   Persona de   Mexicanos en
- Jefe de familia   • Ausentes   migrante   bajos recursos   Nueva York
- Paisano   siempre
                       presentes

Figure 3.4 Reactions to Identities among Mexican Immigrants in New York.

social programs among federal agencies. In sum, after putting these terms to the focus groups, our participants said that they were most comfortable being called *Mexicanos en Nueva York*.

Two other key insights from the focus groups: one participant looked at SP the way he looked at insurance for his cell phone. While he never actually used the insurance on the phone because he took care of it, he knew that he had it if needed: *pero se puede utilizar, para eso sirve pre-afiliarse* ("but it can be used; that is what pre-enrollment is for"). Immigrants also responded positively to the idea presented in the script that they might want to *pre-afiliate* (pre-enroll) with SP so that they could get needed medical care when they returned to Mexico on vacation or family visits. Some suggestions:

> *Tú puedes proteger a toda la familia y todos somos "elegibles." Y cuando vuelvas puedes tener seguro y atención médica* ("You can protect the whole family and we're all eligible. And when you re-turn you can have insurance and medical care").
>
> *Paisano, aprovecha tus vacaciones. Para atenderte y "chequearte." Con suerte tu familia será más saludable, "chequeate" en tu Seguro Popular a bajo costo* ("Countryman, take advantage of your vaca-tion. Get a checkup. Hopefully your family will be healthier. Get a checkup with Seguro Popular at low cost").
>
> *Inmigrante, en tu país hay un Seguro Popular, ya que andas de vacaciones, ya que la familia no tiene seguro, aprovecha para pon-erles un ángel para la salud y cambia para darles una buena salud* ("Immigrant, Seguro Popular is in your country. Since you're on vacation and your family has no health insurance, take this oppor-tunity to give them a guardian angel, to give them good health").

A final, noteworthy observation of the research team at La Unión: sev-eral participants recommended that SP use language and an approach similar to that of St. Jude Children's Hospital in the US, a cancer hos-pital that advertises on Spanish-language TV. Participants remem-bered the tagline in the commercial as *Aquí a todo mundo atendemos, o todo el mundo es atendido aquí* ("Here we take care of everyone, and everyone is taken care of here"). The actual phrase from the video is *En St. Jude ningún niño es rechazado si su familia no puede pagar* (Luis, 2011) ("At St. Jude, no child is turned away because the family cannot pay"). The point is, first, that participants in our focus groups got the message from the St. Jude materials that everyone gets taken care of there, regardless of income; and second, that the SP materials were confusing on such matters.

Consular Focus Groups

We conducted two separate focus groups at the Mexican Consulate, one for men and one for women, to ensure that men and women would be able to talk comfortably about health-related issues. We wanted to compare the results from focus groups outside the consulate with those conducted inside; we were surprised at the number of negative comments about SP we received through focus groups in community organizations. We suspected that people going to the consulate for help would be less openly critical of the consulate and of SP, or might have other reasons for more positive opinions about SP. For example, our SegPop1 results showed that those who had left Mexico more recently had more positive opinions about the government and more positive experiences with SP in their family or friendship networks. We had done nearly half our interviews for SegPop1 at the consulate, and wanted to ensure that we sounded out the same population in our focus groups.

Our procedure for these focus groups was somewhat different from the others. Rather than doing an initial round and then a follow-up, we combined the content for the two focus groups into one, out of practicality. People going to the consulate come once for services (e.g., to get a passport) but are unlikely to return for a second focus group, whereas people return regularly to community organizations, enabling follow-ups. We hence combined the most important parts of the two focus groups into one, as listed in Table 3.1 below.

Women's Consulate Focus Group

The women's focus group had two people with different characteristics. One woman, from Puerto Escondido, Oaxaca, 44, had completed secondary school, had been living in the US for 22 years (NY), and had four US-born children. The second participant, from Atlixco, Puebla, 29, had completed fifth grade, and had been in the US for only four months (NJ). Both were undocumented.

Both women were familiar with SP through third-party accounts or close relatives in Mexico. The more recently arrived woman expressed deep reservations about the program, based upon the experience and poor quality of care that she and her parents had received. She repeatedly asked: why don't they deliver what they promised? The woman who had been in the US for 22 years heard about the program through her in-laws, who were enrolled in the program. She understood the program to be for low-income individuals, indicating that they periodically checked one's income to ensure qualification. She had a sense of the services the program covered and understood that it didn't cover

Table 3.1 Seguro Popular Project (SegPop2) Focus-Group Components and Main Questions, by Phase and Section

Phase 1	Phase 2
I. Knowledge and understanding of Seguro Popular (Conocimiento y comprensión del SP)	I. Reactions to new videos (Reacciones a nuevos videos): Humberto Mayra
a. Have you heard of Seguro Popular? (¿Ha escuchado usted del SP?)	Could you please write the main message of this video? (¿Podrían por favor escribir cuál es el principal mensaje de este video?)
b. What positive experiences have you had, or have you heard that your relatives or friends had? (Qué experiencias positivas han tenido o escuchado usted y sus familiares o conocidos?)	What do Humberto, Mayra, and SP try to say in this ad? Please write your answer first, and when finished we will discuss. (¿Qué es lo que Humberto, Mayra y el SP tratan de decir en este anuncio? Por favor primero escriban su respuesta y cuando terminen las comentamos.)
c. What negative experiences have you had, or have you heard that your relatives or friends had? (¿Qué experiencias negativas han tenido o escuchado usted y sus familiares o conocidos?)	• What do they say? (¿Qué es lo que dicen?) • What don't they say? (¿Qué es lo que no dicen?) • What would you like for them to say? (¿Qué le gustaría que dijeran?)
II. Use of SP (Uso del SP)	What do these ads motivate you to do, or what do they ask you to do? (¿Qué es lo que estos anuncios le motivan a hacer o qué le dicen que haga?)
a. Would you be willing to use it? Explain. (¿Estaría dispuesto a usarlo? Explicar.)	II. On media use (Sobre uso medios de comunicación)
b. Do you recommend it? Explain. (¿Lo recomienda? Explicar)	• TV—How many hours a day do you watch television from Monday to Friday? And on the weekends? What television programs do you watch, at what time, and on what channel? Where do you watch these programs? What time of day is more common for you to watch these programs? (TV—¿Cuántas horas al día ve televisión de lunes a viernes? ¿Y los fines de semana? ¿Qué programas ve en la televisión, en qué horario y en qué canales? ¿En dónde ve estos programas? ¿A qué horas del día es más común que usted vea estos programas?)
c. What information do you need in order to use it? (¿Qué información necesita para usarlo?)	• Radio—How many hours a day do you listen to the radio from Monday to Friday? (¿Cuántas horas al día escucha la radio de lunes a viernes?)...
	• Newspapers (Periódicos)...
	• Internet...?

(*Continued*)

Phase 1

III. Promotional material—reactions (Material promocional—reacciones)

    a. Video on YouTube (Video en YouTube)
    b. Comic (Cómic)
    c. Website (Página de Internet)

IV. Recommendations for the materials (Recomendaciones sobre los materials)

    a. Now that you have more information, are you ready to use or recommend SP? (¿Ahora que tiene más información está dispuesto a usar o recomendar el SP?)
    b. What information is missing? (¿Qué información le hace falta?)
    c. How would you promote it? (¿Cómo lo promocionaría?)

Phase 2

III. Suggestions on scripts, identities, and titles (Sugerencias de scripts, identidades, y títulos)

- I am going to read four promotional texts that could be used to promote the program. Please pay close attention, and, if you'd like, take notes to tell us the words or ideas of each text you like or dislike. We also ask you to suggest how to improve these texts. (A continuación le voy a leer cuatro textos promocionales que podrían utilizarse para promover el programa. Le pido que por favor ponga mucha atención y si lo desea tome notas para que nos diga las palabras o las ideas de cada texto que le gustan o no le gustan. También le pedimos que nos sugiera como mejorar estos textos.)

- Please indicate what identities or titles you identified with most. (Por favor indíquenos con qué identidades o títulos se siente más identificado.)

V. Market analysis of how to reach the Mexican migrant community (Análisis de mercado de cómo llegar a la comunidad migrante mexicana)

a. People you trust about health decisions (Personas en las que confía sobre decisiones de salud)

b. Incentives to use the program (Incentivos para usar el programa)

c. Boosting accessibility (Impulso de accesibilidad)

d. Places to acquire information (Lugares para adquirir información)

e. Media you use and trust (Medios de comunicación que usa y confía)

f. Major sources of information about health (Principales fuentes de información sobre salud)

g. Influential people in health topics (Personas influyentes en temas de salud)

h. Details about consumption information (Detalles sobre consumo de información)

Note: For further details about differences between SegPop1 and SegPop2, see Appendix A.

all illnesses. But she was still unclear about the details and asked if it covered 100% of costs. She had been inquiring about the program on her own, seeking to learn about its services, requirements, and costs, because she thought it important to pre-enroll her entire family. She and her husband were concerned about being deported and wanted to ensure that they were covered, should they have to return to Mexico.

We asked both focus-group members about the promotional materials, including the SP video and comic, and Humberto's and Mayra's videos, to which they reacted differently. When asked whether the promotional materials were useful for their families, the more recently arrived woman was hesitant. Although SP promised these services, she indicated that her family's experiences were different; her father said it would be better to pay for private doctors rather than to suffer waiting for treatment, or perhaps not getting good care. Nonetheless, she said she would try SP, but only for minor issues, not critical illnesses. For her, suspicion that SP wouldn't keep its promise to deliver adequate services remained paramount. The longer-term NYC resident was more receptive to the promotional materials, saying that they inspired her to seek more information about the program and that she would encourage her family in Mexico to use it.

Both felt that there was still a shortage of actionable information. They wanted to know more about how to pre-enroll, what documents were required, addresses of local offices, telephone numbers, and more information about costs. They pointed out that Humberto never stated the location of the facility where his wife had given birth, and that although Mayra was relieved and happy that her family was covered, she never talked about the process or the requirements for SP. Information in the comic seemed to be a good barometer for the level of information needed, and participants appeared more satisfied with it. When asked whether the videos should be longer in order to capture more information, however, they advised against it.

Reactions to the Scripts

Script 4 was considered the best overall, due to its frankness and concrete information about how to obtain or use SP benefits. Participants appreciated that script 4 made clear that not everything was covered and provided insights about where to get help or further information. Participants also supported the promotional language in script 1, saying that it seemed more upbeat and acceptable. Script number 3 was the least favorite. Participants found it judgmental, presuming that Mexicans are *dejados* ("careless"), and it seemed intrusive. They felt as though they were being told what to do in a top-down fashion.

Participants had mixed feelings about the different identities used. The longer-term NYC resident was more receptive to the terms *migrante, paisano, familia migrante,* and *persona de bajos recursos* because she felt that these described who she was. But she noted that they had to be used in a respectful manner. In contrast, the recently arrived woman was uncomfortable with all these terms. Neither woman was receptive to *paisa*—which they thought offensive and vulgar. They identified with *jefe/jefa de familia* and *hijo/hija ausente*, but the latter also brought nostalgia and pain because it underlined how they had to migrate and were separated from their families against their will. They suggested using either Mexicano and/or *hermano/hermana* (brother/sister) when addressing Mexicans living in NY. Lastly, they suggested providing information in community offices, Mexican stores/bodegas, restaurants, and Laundromats.

Men's Consulate Focus Group

Four men were in our focus group, with a mix of backgrounds. All four reported that they were undocumented. Two participants were from Estado de México, one born in 1976 (Participant 1) and the other in 1968 (Participant 4). The other informants were from Puebla (Participant 2), born in 1990, and Oaxaca (Participant 3), born in 1968. Participant 1 had nine years of school, had lived in the US for 19 years, and was currently living in Port Chester, NY. Participant 4 had 11 years of school, and had lived in the Bronx for five years. Participant 2 had nine years of school and had lived for four years in New Jersey. Participant 3 had 12 years of school, had lived in the US for 22 years, and currently resided in New Jersey.

This group was more positive and seemed less suspicious of the government's intent in offering SP. Informants didn't have negative reactions to SP overall but did question clarity, especially what was or wasn't covered, and how and where to use SP or recommend that others use it.

All but one participant (Participant 1) knew something about SP. Participant 2 knew about SP through media coverage and knew that it covered the majority of people; however, his family in Mexico didn't use it. Participant 3 had family members with SP and was under the impression that it covered all types of medical problems, but wasn't sure if there was something it didn't cover.

All informants found the SP promotional videos useful but needed more details. Participant 1 understood that it dealt with health benefits, medicines, and possible coverage for cancer. Participant 2 said it was good but suggested that SP should say more directly what it does and doesn't cover. Participants 3 and 4 similarly suggested using printed material with more details that would otherwise be difficult to communicate through a video. Participant 1 understood that SP offers coverage from the day you're born until death. Participant 2 similarly thought that the video was a kind of life insurance. Participant 3 understood that it was an option if you didn't have private insurance or IMSS or ISSSTE. He liked the videos but suggested that they weren't as clear as they should be, lacking information such as where SP services are located in public health centers. Participants suggested the use of Consulates on Wheels to promote SP from town to town in NY and in Mexico, and perhaps even the use of mobile clinics sponsored by SP. There was also confusion about whether SP was a program like the IMSS or ISSSTE, which, participants reported, have their own clinics. Would an "SP card" permit access to IMSS or ISSSTE clinics or hospitals? Would SP have its own clinics, with the SP logo painted on them like the IMSS or ISSSTE? These questions reflected how these immigrants had lived for some time in NY and hence hadn't seen how SP works in Mexico.

All four liked the comic, seeing it as a good tool to disseminate more detailed information about SP. Yet they repeatedly said that they required more information about what was being promised and what their commitment would be. They wanted to know exactly what to tell their family about cost, coverage, and where to go if they needed SP. The four men generally liked the videos featuring Mayra and Humberto, but further complained about the lack of information and detail in them, asking again whether SP has its own clinics like the IMSS and ISSSTE. They did say that these two videos motivated them to look for more information.

Reactions to the Scripts

In general, the four men were less critical of the identities used to connect with immigrants in the scripts. Yet the theme of actionable information again rose in this group. Participants reported that script 1 made them feel as though *pre-afiliation* (pre-enrollment) could give them peace of mind if they returned to Mexico, but they still had questions about where to go and whether it was the same as IMSS. They liked script 2, saying it was oriented toward *gente mayor* ("older people") and to *nuestra familia* ("our family"), and got that it was directed at *estas personas aquí y sus familias que están allá* ("the people here and their families over there") in Mexico. They didn't object to *paisano* or *paisa* (short for "countryman") or *la familia*, and didn't note the nostalgia this had provoked among previously discussed focus-group members. They reported that the text motivated them to look for more information but also saw this lack of detail as its weakness. Since script 3's main message was to tell them to pre-enroll in case they went back to Mexico, that *puedes contar con SP cuando regreses* ("you can count on SP when you return"), they were surprised that one could pre-enroll while still in the US rather than having to sign up in Mexico. Once again, they highlighted that there wasn't enough information about how to do this.

Script 4 was this group's favorite. The men liked that one could *saber que puede regresar y tener seguro* ("know that one could return and have health insurance") in Mexico. They underscored how helpful it was to know from this text that everything wasn't covered. They thought that this honest admission treated them like responsible adults. But they thought that they still lacked the actionable information they needed: *Sabemos que no todo está cubierto. Pero todavía no sabemos qué está cubierto … Entendemos que no puede cubrir todo—no tienen aparatos adecuados para todo. Pero me gusta que está más completa la información. Es un poco más específica* ("We know that not everything is covered. But we still don't know what's covered …. We understand that everything can't be covered—they don't have a system adequate for all. But I like that there's more complete information. It's a little more specific").

The first author asked if they favored this script because it discussed SP as a policy covering certain things and didn't present it as a social right implying that all health issues were covered all the time for everyone. They said that it made sense to them that it was a policy; *mejor como un póliza, para que sepamos … uno tiene pagar por su parte, también. … Que bueno que especifiquen—para saber que hay límites* ("Better as an insurance, so that we know … one has to pay for some things, too. …. Better if they specify—to know there are limits"). They also responded that this should be part of the initial framing of SP outreach and advertisements. When asked for suggestions, the men urged *que la gente pueden saber que es un póliza, y que esta cuesta. Que es una ayuda, no es gratis. …. Pero hay algún tipo de gente que lo va querer gratis* ("that people should know that it's an insurance, and that it costs something. That it helps, but isn't free. …. But still, some people will want it for free"). Having a clearer understanding that this was a policy rather than a universal right suggested limits to the program's nature, which seemed to make the men less skeptical about the government keeping its word.

Themes

Several themes emerged from the consular focus groups and community-based focus groups. Our intuition that those in the consular focus groups would be less openly critical of SP and the government was supported, likely due to several factors, including a reluctance to criticize the government or SP while in the consulate, or a general difference in orientation between those who are settled in the US and involved in community organizations seeking to change larger systems (e.g., those in La Unión or Masa) versus those not as settled or not seeking systematic change through an organization (Centro del Inmigrante, consulate groups). These differences also manifest themselves in the slightly more positive assessment in the consular focus groups versus the community-based focus groups for some of the identities presented. For example, men in the consular focus group didn't mind the terms *paisano* or *paisa*; those in the community-based focus groups and women in the consular group didn't support them at all.

Beyond these small differences, the general findings about SP were essentially the same across all groups. All participants wanted more actionable texts: information that would allow them to take concrete steps, make decisions, and offer advice to relatives in Mexico. They wanted to know where to get such information, how to contact people who had this information, and what exactly to tell their relatives in Mexico to do. Moreover, all groups thought that SP was a good program, and their appreciation of it rose *when it was presented as an insurance policy rather than as a social right, which, in their minds, implied unlimited coverage for all health conditions and highlighted the broken Mexican social contract that had forced them to migrate in the first place.*

Script 4 was the most popular in all focus groups because it stated that SP was a limited policy and that immigrants had to investigate its specifics before informing their families in Mexico about it or making health care decisions. These findings bring us back to the literature on health-care decision making discussed earlier, which underscores how most people make health care decisions without full information about their treatment options or their illnesses. Respondents in these focus groups supported the fourth script the most because it reduced the uncertainty of their decision making and pointed them to where they could receive needed materials.

Media Use for All Five Focus Groups

To deepen our understanding of what types of media channels might be most effective in reaching Mexicans in NY with information about SP, we asked focus-group participants about their media use. Table 3.2 below summarizes media use across all our groups. Several trends stand

Table 3.2 Media Use by Mexicans in New York for Seguro Popular Project (SegPop2) Television

Focus groups	El Centro del Inmigrante (Staten Island)	La Unión (Brooklyn)	Masa (Bronx)	Mexican Consulate (All men)	Mexican Consulate (All women)
Weekday Hours, Time of Day	Two participants watch TV 1–2 hours daily, 8–9 pm (soap opera) and 11 pm (nightly news on channel 41 or 47)	• Husband: 3.5 hours per day of TV, weekdays: 6–10 am • Wife: 6 hours, weekday, 8–10 am; 6–11 pm • Construction worker: 1 hour weekdays • Airport employee: 7 hours soap opera, 7–8 pm weekdays • Community leader: 2 hours, 7–9 pm	Participant 1: 5 hours daily, AM news (Galavision), PM news (Univision) Participant 2: 2 hours daily, 7 am (Galavision); 6 pm or 7 pm news (Univision) Participant 3: 10 hours weekly, 5–6pm (Univision)	Participant 1–3 hours daily, 7–10 am Participant 2: 2 hours daily, 8am and 7/8 pm Participant 3: 1 hour daily, 6 pm Participant 4: 2 hours daily, 7–10 pm	Participant 1: Half-hour daily when not working; soap opera, 8–9 pm
Weekend Hours, Time of Day	Two participants averaged 4–5 hours on weekends	• Husband: 12 hours, weekend • Wife: 4 hours • Construction worker: 3 hours, weekends • Airport employee: 2 hours weekends; 9–11 am Saturdays • Community leader: 2 hours	Participant 1: No television on weekends Participant 2: No television on weekends, "go out" on weekends Participant 3: No television on weekends	Participant 1: 3 hours Participant 2: No TV Participant 3: 2 hours Participant 4: 2–3 hours	Participant 1: Doesn't watch TV, works

(Continued)

Focus groups	El Centro del Inmigrante (Staten Island)	La Unión (Brooklyn)	Masa (Bronx)	Mexican Consulate (All men)	Mexican Consulate (All women)
Channels	Two participants watched sports on weekends (soccer or boxing on channels 41, 47, 41.2)	• Husband: Galavision and channels 41, 68, 47 • Wife: Univision 41, Galavision, Telemundo 47 • Construction worker: Univision 47, Telemundo, TV-Azteca, Galavision, 68 Telefutura, news at 11pm • Community leader: multiple channels, 7–9pm.			"Canal de las estrellas" (or channel 2)—Televisa and other Mexican channels; watches news, soap operas, and cartoons
Locations	Home	Home	Home	Home	Home
Radio	One participant listened to radio while riding to work in employer's car, 8–10am and 2–3pm, usually music or news in English on 97.9, 101.1. Another participant sometimes listened to radio at work, when allowed, on 92.7.	• Husband: Radio weekdays at work, 7 am and 3 pm • Wife: No radio • Construction worker: Half-hour weekdays, 1 hour weekends, "La Que Buena," "La Mega" • Airport employee: Only weekends, 2 hours, "Radio Wado," "Programa Tu Dinero" (by Radio Cadena Univision)" • Community leader: No radio	Participant 1: Very little but sometimes 11–12 pm, "La Que Buena," 92.7 Participant 2: 2 hours weekly, 3–4 pm, "La Que Buena," 92.7	Participants sometimes listen to "La Que Buena," 92.7, in car, mornings	Neither participant really listens to radio; occasionally at work, participant 1 tunes into and participant 2 tunes into 93.7 when driving

Internet					
	• One participant (55-year-old who immigrated from Mexico DF six years ago) used Internet half-hour daily—mostly Facebook to chat with son in Mexico • Another participant used Internet about 6 hours weekdays, mostly email as part of work but also to connect on Facebook	• Wife: Doesn't know how to use Internet, but her kids help her look at videos and photos of family on Facebook • Construction worker: Used Internet just to check email on his phone • Airport employee: 1 hour daily, to check email, horoscopes, YouTube, stocks; uses Internet more on phone, not home computer • Community leader: 10 minutes daily, 1 hour per week, mostly email	Participant 1: 2–3 hours daily, Facebook, Twitter, and email. Uses it to check the news, etc.; 3 hours weekends, on cell phone. Participant 2: All day sporadically at work on Facebook, 3 hours total. Uses it for Facebook, Univision, to see what's going on, current affairs. Four hours downloading and listening to music, etc., on the weekends, uses home computer and phone the same. Participant 3: Doesn't use Internet	Participant 1: 1 hour daily, at home, on cell phone, Facebook, no email Participant 2: 2 hours daily, on cell phone, very little email, more on weekend Participant 3: 4–5 hours, at home, on cell phone, Facebook and email. Not so much on weekends. Participant 4: No Internet	Participant 1: Half-hour occasionally, at night. On phone, at home, usually to look up songs. Participant 2: About 3 hours per week, mostly to check email, Facebook, or to see videos on YouTube

(Continued)

Focus groups	El Centro del Inmigrante (Staten Island)	La Unión (Brooklyn)	Masa (Bronx)	Mexican Consulate (All men)	Mexican Consulate (All women)
Newspaper	Most popular newspaper among group: Diario de México Edición USA However, they only read it at the community center and rarely bought it themselves. One participant said he would buy it when he knew something to do with the community center or relevant to the Mexican community was to be published. Another participant mentioned reading the Staten Island Advance or the New York Times sometimes	• The newspaper was the principal source of print information for the group, mainly Diario de México Edición USA • Construction worker: the only person who bought and read Diario de México Edición USA newspaper daily	Participant 2: Diario de Mexico Edition USA and El Diario la Prensa but very little, only when her child is in school (other participants don't read the paper with any frequency)	Participants said they read Diario de Mexico Edition USA Participant 1: 2 times per week Participant 2: Buys it when he has time in the morning Participant 3: 2–3 times per week Participant 4: 1 time per week	Both seldom read the newspaper but occasionally read the free community newspapers

Note: For further details about differences between SegPop1 and SegPop2, see Appendix A.

out. First, *Diario de México* was the most mentioned paper, and for many, the only one they read. Second, respondents reported watching the same television channels, including Galavision, Univision Canal 41, Telemundo Canal 47, and Univision Canal 68. They also listened to the same radio stations, including 97.9, 101.1, and 92.7 Programa Tu Dinero (by Radio Cadena Univision). The news was the most widely watched program, indicating that free news coverage would be a fruitful approach for SP in outreach. As one might think, sports, especially *fútbol* (soccer), were most popular with the men. Men and women both reported regularly watching *telenovelas*.

A surprising finding was the relatively high use of the Internet, via cell phone and computer, and use of email, texts, and Facebook (FB) and its related functions. Three of the four men in the consular focus group reported regular use of the Internet. Participant 1 used the Internet one hour daily at home and on his cell phone, mainly to check FB and other websites. Participant 2 used the Internet one hour daily, on his cell phone and more on the weekends. Participant 3 used the Internet four to five hours daily on his phone for FB and email but not as much on weekends. Participant 4 didn't have access to the Internet but would use it if he did.

Community Leaders' Opinions

Building from the results of SegPop1, we thought it important to talk to community leaders. Below, we report results from interviews with three community leaders who offered varying perspectives on SP and the larger relationship between the Mexican government and immigrants. These were largely open-ended interviews, asking about leaders' experience with SP, if they had any clients dealing with SP, and their beliefs about recommending the program to clients. We were open to emergent themes in the interviews (Smith, 2006), e.g., leaders contrasting their knowledge of NY's hospital system with their uncertainty about SP.

The three cases presented below offer differing perspectives. The first was critical of SP and the Mexican government, and knew the health care system in NY well. The second was open to SP's benefits but worried about misunderstandings and cracks in the program. The third focused on the vulnerabilities that immigrants faced in their health care decisions when they had to return to Mexico because of illness. All three leaders focused on cases that occupied most of their attention with SP: sick immigrants who were considering returning to Mexico or staying in the US for treatment.

Leader A: Skepticism about SP

Leader A, head of a community organization that routinely made referrals of sick Mexicans to various NYC hospitals, was skeptical of the motives behind SP and the real options it offered sick immigrants. This leader's perspective seemed to emerge from a generally critical stance on the government and from discussions with immigrants and extensive knowledge about care options in NY. This leader argued that SP was really an attempt to package the *sexenio* (six-year administration) of President Calderón in a positive light, so that audiences would see SP as the president's "main accomplishment."

Leader A reported that immigrants who had sought medical care from SP or had relatives who had done so hadn't had good experiences. Sometimes they were made to wait a long time to be seen, only to be told that they had to pay for tests or go to another hospital, often private, to be seen by a specialist. This leader believed that SP doctors sometimes sent patients on to other hospitals when they should have been attending to them. Leader A, whose organization dealt regularly with NY's public hospitals (in the Health and Hospitals Corporation network), said that staff at the organization knew how to refer sick immigrants for specialty treatment here, and underlined that the treatments were always free or low-cost for the immigrants. What should I do, Leader A asked, if I have a sick immigrant: send the patient back to Mexico, where SP may not cover him/her, or tell the patient to stay in NY, where HHC will definitely cover him/her?

This leader understood SP as a social right for all Mexicans, as unlimited in its guarantees and said that if one could take one's SP card and go to any hospital in Mexico, even an IMSS or ISSSTE one, then SP would be truly keeping the promise that it was making. Unless SP was more comprehensive, this leader couldn't recommend that immigrants use it.

Leader B: Ambivalence about SP

Leader B, who had extensive experience in negotiating the health care system in NY on behalf of immigrant clients of the organization, approached the idea of recommending SP to immigrants as a logistical and moral question: how could I recommend that they go back to Mexico if I'm unsure that the program works and will cover them? This leader reported that the experience of going to the consulate in NY negatively affects how immigrants in the state think about how SP will work, contrasting it with the experience of NY's public (HHC) hospitals: "In New York, you can visit an HHC-affiliated hospital and walk out paying only $15 for your visit and $2 for your medicine. At non-HHC hospitals, you pay on a sliding scale, beginning at $40 for a doctor's appointment." Leader B noted that, while you have to wait, you always leave with medicine if you're sick. The leader remarked that immigrants who go to the consulate report waiting long times for service, and feel they're treated rudely by consular staff and don't always get what they need there. Since they go to the consulate only every "four or five years" for documents, this negative experience sticks with immigrants. But Leader B pointed out that the consulate's treatment of immigrants "has improved," and, in particular, praised the Consulate on Wheels for bringing the consulate closer to the community.

Despite skepticism, Leader B recommended that people use SP but as a "good program of last resort" for anyone who was very sick and needed to return home to get the social and medical support that Mexico offers. Yet the leader highlighted that this is a very labor-intensive, clumsy process to help such a person, requiring hours of community-leader involvement, including visits to the consulate to ensure that it follow through. Recommending people was further complicated by two factors: immigrants believe that the program promises to cover everything; and immigrant leaders don't actually know what's covered and what's not, and find the website hard to navigate.

This leader recognized that SP offers positive, concrete benefits to many immigrant families and recommended that SP do targeted outreach to immigrants, giving them information including

> concrete examples and clear directions with clear costs. ... My biggest suggestion is to stop focusing on enrollment, the larger program itself, and focus on specific things that SP covers and that are in high demand, and costly for the community here and back in Mexico.

The leader suggested targeted questions such as: does someone in your family have diabetes or another illness? Leader B thought that these specifics would make the program more real to immigrants and their families.

Leader C: Vulnerabilities of Immigrants

Leader C focused primarily on the bureaucratic cracks through which immigrants can sometimes fall when moving with an illness from the US to Mexico, and the potential for serious exploitation that sometimes results. Leader C dealt with transfer cases and underscored how critical it is for immigrants to have clear information in that process. Prior to departing for Mexico, patients must have specific names, telephone numbers, and addresses of persons in medical institutions in Mexico that could help them manage their conditions. Establishing these relationships was time-consuming and difficult. The leader believed that such work would be greatly facilitated by opening a Ministry for the Diaspora, or at least an office within SP that would be in charge of relations with the diaspora.

Leader C referred to cases profiled in social media and in the *New York Times*, where migrants had to return to Mexico after the closure of a clinic in Georgia where they'd been receiving treatment. Some with kidney disease returned to a lack of coverage, or to insufficient coverage. In one case, money raised for a kidney transplant had to be used instead for routine dialysis, decreasing chances for a transplant. In another case, a family couldn't afford to pay for the three weekly dialysis treatments needed, and the patient died, as did others (Sack, 2009).

Leader C disturbingly cited a for-profit company that is now consulting with medical institutions, community organizations, and consulates across the US, which tells hospitals that are supporting Mexican immigrants with serious illnesses that it will help "take them off your hands" by transferring them back to Mexico. According to this leader, a seriously ill immigrant was transported back to Mexico, promised that a public program (presumably, SP) would pay for the needed treatments. After two months, the patient, who had been transferred to a private hospital, was thrown out of that hospital. Leader C believed that the for-profit company receives a transfer fee for each immigrant and that some immigrants are transferring back to Mexico and into medical situations where they're not getting the care that they need or were promised. Governments should take this situation seriously. First, it negatively affects the lives of those immigrants involved and offers apparently ill-gotten gains to this for-profit company. Second, such negative processes and outcomes can work against programs like SP, even if they have nothing to do with it.

Notes

1 The second part of this book draws on our report "How to Talk to Mexicans in New York about El Seguro Popular" (Smith et al., 2012), subcontracted to Baruch College, School of Public Affairs, with the Centro de Investigación y Docencia Económica (CIDE) in Mexico City. Appendix A summarizes the main characteristics of SegPop1 and SegPop2 projects. Hereafter, we refer to the survey data and report as SegPop1 (Smith & Seguro Popular Team, 2012) and the focus-group and interview research reported below as SegPop2 (Smith et al., 2012).

2 We selected this YouTube video (www.youtube.com/watch?v=0LCXO rAdgu0) because it was one of the most viewed on the Internet, with more than 33,000 views when we organized the focus groups.

3 See Table 3.1 for focus-group components and our main questions by phase and section.

4 Even common terms in public affairs such as "sustainability" have been found to have wildly different meanings across sectors. Research shows that many in the developing world associate the term with "neocolonialism"; in nongovernmental organizations, it's often perceived as a "panacea"; and in resource management, audiences routinely see it as a "quaint but unattainable ideal" (Rice & Robinson, 2013, p. 234).

5 We wrote the scripts with the idea that SP was intended for persons with low incomes (*de bajos recursos*) because this is what our informants in NY believed, although this isn't precisely true. All persons not otherwise covered by insurance in Mexico are eligible to be covered by SP, regardless of income. Most people not otherwise covered by an insurance plan are *de bajos recursos* (and many immigrants understood this to be so). Note that we presented the scripts in this research as tools not approved or endorsed by SP, and we employed a few terms in "Spanglish" used by the Mexican immigrant community, such as *elegibles* and *chequearte*. Additionally, we're aware that some Spanish-speaking immigrants might use *pólizas* to refer to *políticas*, even though we ensured that focus-group participants understood that, by *póliza*, we meant "insurance policies"; and by *políticas*, we meant public or governmental "policies."

4 Concluding Strategies for Communicating with Immigrants

Building from our focus-group research in the second part of the Seguro Popular (SP) project and relevant social marketing literature, we develop five interconnected strategies to promote a more accurate understanding of SP and similar initiatives. We highlight what more motivating, actionable strategies could be implemented with transnational Mexican communities and in comparable campaigns. These recommendations discuss the theoretical underpinnings of each argument and provide concrete "to do" steps for promoting the use of SP and similar programs. These lessons can be applied, in modified form, to other areas of diasporic bureaucracies. They could also promote the positive integration of immigrants into US institutions, to be used in interactions between immigrants and US schools, local governments, and related institutions: these contributions are intended to be portable. We include one recommendation specifically on expanding outreach and enrollment of *Los Otros Dreamers*: Mexicans who grew up in the US and were deported back to Mexico, and their US-citizen children who returned with their parents or siblings when they were deported. Together, they number more than one million in Mexico.

Promote a Clearer Idea of What Seguro Popular Is, So That It Is Not Rejected for What It Is Not

The single most important issue arising from our research involved the conflicting perceptions and experiences that our research participants shared about SP. Seguro Popular presented itself as a "social right" for all Mexicans. This echoed other government pronouncements, e.g., a 2011 report on human rights in Mexico proclaiming the government's goal to "make real the right to health" (SRE, 2011a). In the context of SP, many immigrants and their leaders understood the term "social right" as promising that everyone was always covered under all conditions, for free. But in practice, SP offered an insurance policy to everyone who wasn't otherwise covered, a policy with incomplete coverage.

Ironically, SP *had* accomplished something very important: to offer, or at least make a reasonable attempt at offering, minimum health-insurance coverage to Mexico's entire population. But the *perception* remained that the government wasn't to be trusted. *This led to an unnecessary dynamic in which SP was sometimes rejected for not being a panacea, instead of embraced as a much better medical-insurance program than previously existed.* It was rejected for not being all-encompassing rather than embraced for offering everyone something. This problem can be alleviated by providing unequivocal clarity across communications about what exactly is "free" or simply "low-cost."[1] Much SP messaging conflated these two concepts in ways that our focus groups described as off-putting and lacking in credibility. If audiences find such messaging unclear or confusing, they cannot be expected to enlist in SP or similar health care programs.

From a social marketing perspective, this problem relates directly to how the *behaviors* that SP messaging targeted weren't always clear. The overarching question that should be asked of every SP promotional material, whether online or in forms like brochures is: what does SP want audiences to *do* as a result of seeing these materials? The answer should always be framed in terms of increasing or decreasing certain actions (Lee & Kotler, 2016). Focus-group results showed that immigrants were unclear about where they were supposed to go and what was available—i.e., what action they should take to learn more about SP or to start receiving services. At a minimum, what behaviors need increased, decreased, modified, or sustained serious attention in SP marketing? Any chosen behaviors should be easy to act on, as informants' complaints in focus groups confirmed.

Some SP promotional materials did provide actions–e.g., SP's website highlighted an enrollment section with a phone number to call. As mentioned earlier in this book, a behavior isn't a message but helps define, give purpose to, and prioritize the final messages that one might find in, say, video advertising. If, as we suspect, getting one to "tell" one's family about SP is a core behavior for the campaign, efforts should target and measure the increase or decrease in that particular behavior along all fronts. A more integrated, behaviorally focused social marketing design for SP, specific to each medium, could drive visitors to "like" the Facebook page only as it pertains to showing others on individuals' newsfeed that they're affiliated with SP. More than "awareness" can be created through such messaging. For example, an

SP Facebook page post on October 8, 2012, stated, "Breast cancer does not discriminate based upon age, race, or social status, no woman is free from danger, carelessness is deadly." Aside from what the vague term "carelessness" is intended to prohibit, the comment doesn't appear to target a behavior and is what the social scientific literature describes as a "fear appeal" without a necessary, concrete recommendation to accompany it (Witte, 1992). It didn't tell readers, for example, to do one key action: get a breast-cancer screening.

A belief emerging in focus groups (whether true or not) was that SP had too many requirements. An assumption that getting into SP could be a forbidding process was enough to turn many away. So, messaging should focus on the one to three steps, at most, that it might take to get free or low-cost health care. All SP campaigns should highlight how "easy" it is to be part of SP by doing X, Y, or Z. Model examples of making it "easy" to engage in a behavior include Amazon.com's 1-Click Ordering system (Heath & Heath, 2010) and NYC's move to a 311 number that helped residents know what number to call for all nonemergency problems in the city (Lee & Kotler, 2011). SP's marketing efforts needed to focus on similar, simple behaviors that create perceptions of ease and accessibility.

SP needed to be "repositioned" for transnational audiences. Positioning is a social marketing concept describing "the act of designing the organization's actual and perceived offering in such a way that it lands on and occupies a distinctive place in the mind of the target audience— where you want it to be" (Lee & Kotler, 2011, p. 218; Ries & Trout, 1986). Repositioning takes the perceived offering to a new, distinctive place in your audience's minds. The focus groups identified much confusion about what was distinctive about SP in relation to Mexican federal government programs, such as the difference between IMSS and SP. A positioning statement attending to the following considerations would establish better campaign communication with immigrants: "We want [target audience] to see [desired behavior] as [set of benefits] and as more important and beneficial than [competition]" (Lee & Kotler, 2011, p. 218). All marketing and communication efforts are enhanced by highlighting not only what's unique about SP (including incentives) in comparison with other actions that audiences may take, but also the *costs* of alternative behaviors (i.e., not using SP for one's health care). Highlighting how easy SP or similar programs are to access could be a major part of repositioned communication—e.g., "Compared with every other public health care system in the world, SP is the easiest to sign up for and receive treatment quickly." Suggestions for other campaign behaviors are provided below.

Use More Networked, Broader Outreach Methods to Engage Structures of Local and Transnational Immigrant Life

By "networked" approaches, we mean that SP and similar outreach efforts should move more from "vertical," top-down methods such as video commercials coming directly from the government to citizens, to more lateral, "horizontal" strategies that leverage existing stakeholders, leaders, and close friendships to promote programs like SP to target audiences. We found that much of immigrants' transnational lives and their links between those in the US and those in Mexico took place at the *municipio* (municipal) level. Immediate and extended families are the basic building blocks of transnational life. Hometown associations (HTAs) or *clubes de oriundos* of a *municipio* or a section of a *municipio* follow. Formal or informal political parties or political cliques also organize transnationally (e.g., for fundraising). In the case of how Mexicans in the US would best understand political structures, municipal-level organizations are then scaled up at the federation level, where clubs from a whole state organize.[2] The key lesson is *that there currently exist myriad potential channels through which correct information about SP and similar programs might flow and get to immigrants and their families.* These channels could be used to ask people to take concrete, actionable steps—e.g., enroll in the program. Below, we consider how these approaches may be implemented through specific media, while our third conclusion targets underused face-to-face communication and marketing strategies.

Traditional Media Channels

Given our focus-group findings, we advise SP and similar programs to provide more convergence between various media platforms. By developing more networked outreach methods, SP could use a variety of channels and messengers to communicate key messages, incorporating but also surpassing traditional approaches to advertising. Our focus groups confirmed that SP should target the newspapers and radio and TV stations already identified in this book during the days and times participants provided (particularly through TV news, sports, and *telenovelas*). Outdoor advertising in NY areas where our target populations live and work could be used, too, such as on public transportation, billboards, or posters. Pinpointing ads at the local level is far more cost-effective than approaches attempting to saturate a wider market. Strong visual materials should be used on flyers and brochures, as focus groups reported that some audiences may be illiterate. Our participants highlighted the centrality of *Diario de México* as the main newspaper they read; pinpointing such publications should be integral to further outreach.

Nearly a hundred years ago, Robert E. Park highlighted the immigrant press as an institution that could aid integration into the US (Park, 1922). Newspapers should hence be a critical part of a coordinated media outreach strategy to the Mexican community. One focus-group participant recommended that we take out a "good *periodicazo*" ("advertisement") with all the details and information about SP, which people could read and hang on to for future reference.

Entertainment Media

Beyond traditional media strategies, and consistent with a social marketing approach, our groups confirmed the importance of working with entertainment media to promote SP. Comic strips can continue to tell real stories about Mexicans who have used SP successfully, with clear, direct information about what readers should *do*. Many focus-group participants (men as well as women) noted watching *telenovelas*. Aside from running SP commercials during *telenovelas*, we recommend an entertainment-education campaign that includes SP promotional content *within telenovela* programming (Entertainment Education, 2012; Kennedy et al., 2009). Existing entertainment-education efforts like "Nuestro Barrio" have been tremendously successful in leveraging entertainment media toward public causes (Lee & Kotler, 2011, p. 123).

SP and similar programs should work with writers and producers of popular entertainment media to develop plotlines providing clear information about access to and potential uses of programs like SP for transnational populations. Sports channels, especially those covering soccer and boxing, would provide critical opportunities to advertise. Using a similar strategy, SP content should be included *in* ads and, if resources exist, in messages by commentators during such programming. One might use, e.g., Dr. Chapatín, a popular Mexican TV character whose famous comedy show originated in the 1980s. Programs like SP might consider inserting content in media such as Spanish-language video games distributed in localities. It may come as a surprise to many, but Baranowski et al. (2008) completed a meta-analysis of 25 studies that used video games to address health behavior outcomes (e.g., exercise, diet) and *found benefits/ gains in almost all of them* (cited in Rice & Atkin, 2013, p. 12). The effectiveness of these platforms shouldn't be ignored in creating a multifaceted communication strategy around programs like SP.

Text Messaging

The focus groups confirmed that text messaging would be useful for priority audiences to receive information about SP. Text-messaging campaigns in health care are finding great success around the world. Fogg and Adler (2009) provide an example of measured, successful text messaging in obesity and other health campaigns (see also Lefebvre, 2009). In India, one children's health program, Radiophone (sponsored by Sesame Street Workshops), has been influential with rural populations who don't have televisions. Program administrators gave cell phones to target audiences to receive radio broadcasts; a pilot program with 31 episodes started in 2011 and has connected with more than 200,000 listeners (Helping, 2012, para. 4). Results showed that "by combining local radio, mobile technology and engaging Sesame education ... critical information [was delivered] to families whose health may depend on it" (para. 9).

SP and comparable campaigns could use the ubiquity of cell phone technologies to create text-message blasts for audiences. A more behavioral focus for SP messaging could be forwarded by making "text to this number to receive more information" a primary action. After participants' cell phone numbers are received and opted into, SP updates could be periodically sent with relevant information. Immigrants often receive direct advertisements to their cell phones that they find useful. These blasts might be coordinated with links to "like" or further engage with the Facebook (FB) page, with an option for automatic updates about SP to the cell phone number. After such a channel is open, repeat messages could reinforce correct information about the program at a low cost. Three examples could be:

Dear Mexicans in NY: Be like Humberto/Mayra and sign up for Seguro Popular! Seguro Popular gives you the information needed to help your family's health in Mexico. Go to [website] for more information about his/her experience and your options.

Dear Mexicans in NY: Be like Humberto/Mayra. Pre-enroll with SP before your vacation, and do that doctor's visit in Mexico. Go to [website] for more info about his/her experience and your options.

Dear Mexicans in NY: Know someone with a serious illness? Have that person explore treatment options in Mexico with SP. Go to [website] to learn about Humberto/Mayra, who was helped by SP, and to learn about your options.

Ideally, each of these texts could lead to local websites for immigrants, e.g., of community organizations or their *municipios*. Various analytics, especially A/B testing, could test different versions of these messages to take the guesswork out of which version(s) increase enrollments in the program (see also Waisanen, Hahn, & Gander, 2019).

The Seguro Popular Website

In all our focus groups, subjects reported conflicting, sometimes ambivalent, responses to SP's website. They thought it offered too much detail on things that they didn't need or want and not enough information on what they wanted to know about—especially who was covered, the conditions covered, and any associated costs. The search box on the website didn't function well. When the first author typed *cobertura* ("coverage"), "cancer," and "asthma" in the search box, and pressed *ir* ("go"), no results appeared for any of these searches. While there were other ways to investigate these topics on the website, e.g., through Mi Seguro Popular, the search box is one of the most likely tools that people will use. In both sets of focus groups, subjects didn't find the SP website user-friendly. Nor did they find the catalog by SP, CAUSES (or Catálogo Universal de Servicios de Salud), to be helpful.

Part of the problem was that SP's website was loaded with excellent outreach information, but few immigrants actually went to it. The *historias de vida* ("life histories") are well done, with attractive photos and videos of the people being described, all of whom had compelling stories. But these stories were buried deep within the website. This problem is common in current site design and development—leaders of organizations and agencies grow enamored of adding more and more content to their sites when, in effect, a move toward greater simplification is what audiences need to find a website useful.

Some researchers have described this problem as "auto-communication" (Cheney et al., 2011, pp. 133–134). Just as poets tend to be the most discerning readers of their own poems, organizations can easily fall in love with their communication, promoting an "organizational narcissism" that cuts the institution off from important information from external audiences (p. 134). The organization itself effectively becomes the *primary* audience for its messages. So, institutions must be brutally honest about what real audience reactions are to their materials. In state-of-the-art work on websites, research findings about videos in health care campaigns have been clear—"agencies' efforts should focus on creating one quality video to place on a homepage [i.e., not multiple videos that are really only of interest to the organization], as video views declined the deeper people navigated into the site" (Perrault & Silk, 2014, p. 20).

One key would be to get a few stories circulating through social networks of immigrants by their own energy (see social media strategies below). We would advise using a separate page that would appear on a search labeled "Mexicanos en Nueva York y Seguro Popular." Information for immigrants by state of origin in Mexico would be useful, with phone numbers or other relevant contact information for local hospitals and clinics, and information listed by state of destination in the US and phone numbers and hours of operation for the consulates and Health Windows.

"Age" and "cost" criteria appeared to be far more complex than necessary on SP's website. This is related to our first conclusion about communicating simply and accessibly about who and what is covered through SP. On SP's website, the section "medical coverage" listed different types of level 1 and 2 public service promotions covered. But it was hard to understand the specific age ranges for specialty areas: it stated that "all types of cancers are covered for those under 18" and "transplants for kids under 18"; the next line stated that "the same transplant is covered for people older than 18," and the two following lines said *cáncer de mama* (breast cancer) and "testicular cancer"—but with no age mentioned. It's unclear what's age-specific and what's not. The language randomly attributing under 18, over 18, and, elsewhere, what was blocked for those "over 60" leaves readers wondering what exactly is unique to particular age groups.

Similar comments hold true about areas of the website that listed costs, quotas, or percentages covered. Distilling the information down to single, clear visuals that are consistent across media platforms could have uncluttered SP's website and created more impactful messaging for what SP does. On the website, we consistently found that charts might pertain to one category such as "under 18s" but had a difficult time finding evidence of what was covered for those over 60. In the section called *adultos mayores* ("older adults"), the exact age group that the information was referring to remained unspecified—from information in other areas of the website, it seemed to refer to adults over 60, but this was unclear. In the "SP for me" section, we understood that if individuals weren't covered under a family quota, they must pay a percentage of costs (e.g., 50% of expenses). However, it was unclear, if there was an annual deductible, what additional costs might be incurred for medicines. Or, if an individual's illness was categorized as level 3, did that mean the patient would be covered 100% if a quota was paid? Navigating SP's website, the answers to these questions weren't as immediately apparent as they might be, so we would encourage such programs to clarify, make coherent, and simplify as much information as possible so that audiences have no doubt about what costs are specifically related to age categories.

Many concrete suggestions for improving SP's website and making CAUSES more usable follow the logic outlined so far and can be made clearer by credible comparison websites such as that of the American Red Cross (ARC): www.redcross.org. ARC's website serves different audiences through simple design features and, most important, clear behavioral choices for the exact audiences who visit the site (the most prominent features of the site are tabs up top with specific behaviors like "donate funds," "take a class," "give blood," "get assistance," etc.). SP and similar programs might revise their websites with one easily identifiable tab that opens for "Mexicans in New York" or *Mexicanos en otro país* ("Mexicans in another country"). This site (or tab) should be simple and organized according to types of users. Users have difficulty differentiating between information that may or may not be useful. Such websites should consolidate information—e.g., provide *one* page of core, clear information on diseases and ages covered for potential participants, rather than many separate pages that participants have to guess their way through (Heath & Heath, 2007).

Social Media

Our informants in the first and the second set of focus groups discussed widespread use of Facebook (without prompting from us); and they responded to our questions about whether it would be a good way to reach immigrants. They described using FB in everyday interactions to keep in touch with family in Mexico and elsewhere in the US. Some informants used FB through a home computer, while others used cell phones. SP has a FB page, but incorporating new design features and other updates for it could substantially improve communication about the health care program, especially by incorporating the web-based channels that immigrant communities use. Most sending communities have FB pages to which at least some of their members belong. Sometimes they're sponsored by a municipality and sometimes by immigrant clubs or even groups of adult children of immigrants who participate and maintain the sites. SP could design a FB-based platform with FAQs and other relevant features. Immigrants wouldn't have to look for information about SP but could stumble upon it or be "nudged" (Thaler & Sunstein, 2008) toward it in the online world of transnational life, e.g., it could be embedded into *municipios'* websites or HTAs.

SP and similar programs should systematically link their FB pages to local *municipios* and immigrants' FB groups and other online networks, since immigrant life is organized at the municipal level. If SP invested in creating web-based messages (considering some of the best practices outlined below) that were more user-friendly and attuned to the social dynamics of its priority audiences, its chances for enlisting support would greatly increase—as long-standing social influence strategies support (Cialdini, 2008). Every state health office and major *municipio* could have a designated person(s) to whom questions about SP could be directed, with an email and a phone number. Since SP has presence and personnel in every state and several major *municipios* in the country, this could theoretically be possible. Such a system would encourage more use than the phone access currently provided via complaint lines since (at least in some *municipios*) the designated person or health center, hospital, or clinic would likely be known to immigrants or their families. A major challenge for SP and a limit on the efficacy of this suggestion is that SP doesn't have its own clinics. It relies on the medical and other health infrastructure available to each *municipio*. Hence, greater dissemination of information about SP could increase demand that couldn't be met by existing facilities.[3]

Because negative, inaccurate testimonials about programs like SP can also circulate and be shared, it's worth planning for the possibility that such accounts might "go viral" on the web or social media. Sites like Yelp have increased the monitoring and accountability that organizations face in their work with different publics. Many US businesses have instructed employees to respond quickly to customers' complaints and questions through social media pages. *We're now in an environment where initiatives that don't continually interact with and manage their relationships with constituencies are at a disadvantage.* The goal of public communication should thus be as much to "interact" responsively with members as to simply "broadcast" messages at them. SP's FB page tended to broadcast updates like "The objective of SP is to change the Mexican population to care, conserve, and improve health." Another update from our study period stated, "Children less than five years of age are covered for diseases and preventive care," with a link that led to a "full story"—but when one clicked on the link, it simply led to a Twitter page with the same headline and no further information. Switching from a broadcast to an interactive social media mentality should greatly improve current promotions for initiatives like SP.

We noted a fair bit of negative commentary attached to some YouTube videos. But these sources shouldn't be avoided: to develop better communication strategies, they should be seen as audience objections or "barriers" to be overcome (Weinreich, 2010). First, if negative messages about SP persist, they might identify problems that SP should know about and address—e.g., if there's a persistent report that patients in a particular clinic have been asked to pay for tests or medicines that should be free, SP personnel could quickly investigate and correct incorrect claims. Second, these strings of complaints could be monitored, studied, and addressed to prevent cascading misinformation or online opinion contagions.

Much new research supports these recommendations and provides direction for advancing campaigns like SP. As mentioned, social media are best used less to "broadcast" messages than to develop and maintain interactive relationships with users (Davis, 2012a). Highlighting why such shifts have taken place, Mills (2012) finds that organizations now "have less control over what is being said about their brands, relinquishing the 'voice' of authority to the consumer" (p. 163). Lovett (2011) notes that "it's the interactions with people that constitute the essence of social media" (p. 76). One example: over 90% of people who "like" a FB page never revisit it. Instead, the majority of FB interactions occur through one's "newsfeed"; so, marketers should drive traffic to pages with fresh, involving content from real people working with SP, not unnamed administrators (Davis, 2012a). Attention to users' identities, relationships, groups, and sharing habits should be incorporated into effective social media strategies (Hayden, Waisanen, & Osipova, 2013; Kietzmann et al., 2012; see also Waisanen, 2009; Waisanen, 2011; Waisanen, 2019).

At Blue State Digital (the organization that worked with the 2008 and 2012 Obama campaigns' online efforts in the US), Davis (2012a) found that stories developed for promotional efforts on social media should be consistent (see also Aaker & Smith, 2010; O'Flavahan & Goulet, 2012; Shifman, 2012). And any content created should be highly *sharable*; to increase the social reach of a campaign, share buttons should be added to all online pages. Davis (2012b) discovered that a simple six-word essay contest asking people on FB to tell others about the best teacher they ever had garnered more than 100,000 entries. Some social media research demonstrates that

> content with numbers in [the] title, e.g., list content such as 'Top 10 Ways' or '5 Best Designs,' tend to be shared more on Facebook than those without. The same also applies to content with price or another figure in the title.
>
> (Facebook, 2012a, para. 15)

Similar moves could be made by health programs through contests to describe members' favorite doctor in seven words. Social media can be a source for finding as many success stories about SP, which can then be made into "stories of the day/week." One research group found that "fill-in-the-blank" posts generate about 90% more engagement than the average text post. And an internal study showed that top-performing question ads (those with >0.3% engagement in the form of likes, comments, and shares) are fewer than eight words and offer three concise answer choices (Facebook, 2012b, para. 12). In undertaking social media strategies, posts with fewer than 80 characters have 66% higher engagement, question posts intended to start dialogue with participants have double the response rates of others, and fill-in-the-blank posts generate, on average, nine times more responses than others—so campaigns should consider their audiences as "responders," not "readers" (Barnett, 2011). Digital media practices further underscore how programs like SP should target more specific behavioral choices with their audiences.

"Infographics," rather than purely text-based messages on social media, have also become important in marketing for social causes. Startling statistics about SP could easily be compiled into small but powerful visuals for social media. Research at Kronik Media confirms that "posts that include an image generate about 180% more engagement and posts with a video approximately 120% more engagement than the average post" (Facebook, 2012b, para. 9). The timing for releasing messages to audiences through social media remains a critical part of these strategies: traffic on FB tends to peak from late morning to early afternoon, and midweek posts tend to have higher engagement rates (Barnett, 2011).

Videos for social media campaigns continue to be spotlighted in research. According to Pixability, having a video increases your chance of being on the first Google page by 53 times (Kramer, 2011). One study by Dan Zarella revealed that stories indicating that they had videos were shared far more than average stories on Facebook (Facebook, 2012a). In 2008, "Obama campaign managers posted over 1,800 videos on the YouTube channel, garnering over 110 million views during the election" (Mills, 2012, p. 164). For YouTube videos, one critical recommendation is to *make titles less promotional than informational*, since search engines and humans favor educational content more than advertising (Five, 2012). Videos should be short, with longer ones broken into a numbered series and titled for easy searches—and, consistent with the social marketing approaches adopted in these conclusions, it's best to have clear calls to action in videos (Five, 2012).

SP and comparable campaigns could use social media managers to provide consistent interactions and content with transnational immigrant audiences. One clear advantage of a coordinated social media strategy is that the very success of communication can be tracked by these individuals. Several programs exist for monitoring campaigns, Google Analytics arguably being the most important and cheapest. Another excellent program for measuring success is EdgeRank, which weighs activities such as sharing, liking, and tagging. Another program well suited for larger campaigns is Google URL Builder, which can design customized URLs by channel and post. Various Search Engine Optimization (SEO) strategies, a set of techniques that affect what sites appear in browser searches, may also be of interest. These techniques involve forms of lower artificial intelligence, learning from the direction and redirection of user searches, and adjusting in response to registered patterns.

Use Local Organizations in Immigrant Life to Orchestrate Face- and Place-Based Strategies

Following the last strategy, our research suggested that intensive face-to-face counseling sessions could be organized through the organizations of immigrant life, rather than extended *only* through costly mainstream media campaigns. As described in the SegPop1 report, one-on-one dissemination of information yielded the greatest understanding from participants (Cousineau et al., 2010). This underused campaign strategy was highlighted during the SegPop2 focus groups. Contrary to what many people believe, compared with advertising and other forms of influence, "persuasion is most effective in face-to-face interaction. …. [I]nfluence attempts tend to operate less conspicuously in interpersonal encounters" (Gass & Seiter, 2011, p. 9). These long-standing findings are well known in the communication field but are frequently bypassed in practice. If the choice exists, influence efforts "should definitely choose the interpersonal arena" (Glynn et al., 2004; Wenburg & Wilmot, 1973, p. 28).

Building from our last recommendation, it's critical to meet people where they already are and to work with trustworthy and likable "face-to-face" messengers or "midstream" community leaders such as church leaders and organizers of sports events to provide opportunities to sign up for SP (Gass & Seiter, 2011; Lee & Kotler, 2016). Social norms marketing—which applies perceptions that similar "others" are engaging in targeted behaviors (Lee & Kotler, 2011)—should be used to leverage group pressures toward SP and similar programs.

Focus-group participants provided a perfect example, mentioning that flyers should be distributed around schools, mostly via teachers or parents. Audiences should come into contact with such individuals frequently, and social norms supporting behaviors should be made as *visible* as possible (Lee & Kotler, 2011), planning for social diffusion as part of SP's promotional design (Rogers, 2003).

It's far more effective to leverage existing relationships to promote transnational health care programs than other methods, providing places where target audiences can sell themselves on the idea of SP rather than receive one-way, top-down communication from distant authorities (on the effectiveness of "self-sell" strategies, see Pratkanis & Aronson, 2001). Some focus-group members' concerns that videos might seem propagandistic (with existing skepticisms about what the government may be peddling) underscore the need to use this communication strategy, broadening the trusted messengers, stakeholders, and partners involved with SP. Fishbein and Ajzen's Integrative Model shows three central determinants of behavior change:

> beliefs about the good and bad outcomes of a behavior, beliefs about what important others do and expect the individual to do with regard to the behavior, and beliefs about whether one has the skills and the opportunity to engage in a behavior successfully.
> (Hornik, 2013, p. 40)

By working with existing networks of immigrant influence, all three determinants can dovetail in signing up for programs like SP: the realistic ins and outs of such programs are quickly explained by trusted others who, in turn, spur immigrants' efficacy to use the program.

The same networks of immigrant organizations discussed above could be used to effectively carry out face-to-face sessions. The SegPop1 project conducted more than 800 one-on-one interviews, inside and outside the Mexican Consulate, in only a few months. All these encounters involved a brief explanation of what SP offered, why it was a good idea, and how immigrants and their families would benefit. SP could hire several dozen volunteers (especially college students) for a month or two of weekend days—8 to 16 days of work in one or two summer months—and get them to discuss and distribute literature to people in parks and at churches, sporting events, community organizations, and more. If the supports previously outlined were already in place—e.g., user-friendly and actively managed social media platforms organized via the networks of immigrant life (soccer clubs, *municipios*, committees, HTAs, *clubes de oriundos*, etc.) and more personnel in the Health Windows—the effectiveness of these one-on-one encounters would be enhanced. If each *municipio* had a designated person to answer questions and had links to SP's FB page and these numbers via a *municipio* or club website, including the number of the Health Windows in handed-out materials, a more integrated communication strategy would be established.

One recommendation from the SegPopl report needs reiteration: coordination should take place in any effort to promote SP and similar programs more broadly, with an increase in staff dedicated to such efforts (in SP's case, through the Mexican Consulate in NY). People who can issue invitation messages or reminder phone calls or emails (or automating some of these processes with software) have proved to be helpful in a variety of campaigns (Snyder & LaCroix, 2013, p. 125). As Dorfman and Wallack (2013) spotlight:

> Motivating people to jog in neighborhoods riddled by violence or encouraging consumption of fresh fruits and vegetables where none are available, even if somehow successful in getting people's attention and motivating them to want to change, will do little to improve their overall life chances.
>
> (p. 337)

Similarly, *it's not enough to ask for individuals to change their behaviors (e.g., signing up for SP) if there aren't attendant structural and community changes that increase the likelihood that those behaviors can even happen.*

Consideration should be given to "influential others" who could carry out these one-on-one efforts for SP (Lee & Kotler, 2016): individuals whom target audiences may easily relate to, connect with, or see as credible and trustworthy. In SP's case, one immediate avenue suggested itself: the *tortillero* (tortilla-maker) networks in NY. A small number of Mexican-owned *tortillerías* (tortilla factories) serve the entire NY area with the tortillas that almost every Mexican family eats daily. Deliveries go from house to house, as well as to local *tiendas* (stores). It may be possible to enlist the *tortilleros* to disseminate information with their tortilla deliveries. Another option is to offer community and organizational leaders training in who qualifies for SP and perhaps deputize them to pre-enroll immigrants at their community organizations. Giving community leaders the ability to offer something concrete to their clients would enlist the self-interest of the leaders as leaders, and thus promote their incentive to advocate for SP and related behaviors with primary audiences (on the need to actively pursue people's "self-interest" in campaigns, see Manheim, 2011). We would also recommend considering larger corporate partnerships to promote more cross-sector credibility, reach, and convergence between different types of media and institutions (Jenkins, 2006) but also to appeal to corporate "self-interest" for being involved with socially responsible and civically engaged initiatives.

A communication strategy further suggested by our research in SegPop1 and 2 projects is *piggybacking* (Smith, 2006; Smith & Seguro Popular Team, 2012), as discussed briefly in Chapter 2, which is going to and taking advantage of places where large concentrations of Mexicans would naturally be, so that much literature could be distributed in short periods. Part of a local campaign in NY could include flyers, posters, and comics in schools, in Mexican or non-Mexican organizations that serve Mexicans, and in local stores and other local establishments (*tortillerías, panaderías* [bakeries]; *peluquerías, estéticas* or *salones de belleza* [barbershops or beauty salons]; *taquerías* [taco shops], delis, *farmacias* [pharmacies], *clínicas*, etc.) that include SP basic information. Social marketing theory suggests using material products as part of campaign efforts. Products that act as quick prompts or cues to visit a website, call a phone number, or ask for any other target behaviors should be used, i.e., "visual or auditory aids which remind us to carry out an activity we might otherwise forget" (McKenzie-Mohr & Smith, 2011, p. 71).

The social marketing and social influence literatures unanimously agree that *place* is one of the most important considerations for effective messaging. Indeed, behavioral economics has been almost exclusively devoted to the wealth of evidence behind this strategy (Thaler & Sunstein, 2008). Kammer et al. (2016) state that

> the role of the general environment in which an individual operates should not be underestimated. Health behavior is always embedded in a particular set of circumstances—be they a circle of friends who are smokers, a supportive social network, high alcohol duty, the lack of cycle tracks, or a ban on certain drugs.
>
> (p. 7)

Communication should be targeted to days and times when Mexicans would be in the streets or concentrated for particular events.

In SegPop1, we piggybacked on the September 16 celebrations and the great attendance at soccer and baseball games in Red Hook Park. We found piggybacking to be more effective than, say, simple street distribution, because people want to get home when they get off the subway, and people at soccer games or Independence Day celebrations are already in "party mode," wherein talking to someone for a few minutes doesn't interfere with plans for their day—and might even be seen as a welcome distraction rather than a hindrance to getting home, making dinner, feeding the kids, etc. SP and similar programs could focus on Día de la Vírgen de Guadalupe or other holidays. In NY, we advise using summer days, which are longer; and summer events are likely to be in public, outdoor spaces where access won't be problematic for those distributing the literature.

Place strategies should be used to bring SP information directly to where target audiences work, play, and interact every day. The Consulates on Wheels are a trusted, well-suited mechanism for accomplishing this task; in the US, mobile dental clinics have been a particularly successful example of a similar strategy (Lee & Kotler, 2016). Mobile consulates can ask for specific behaviors at nonprofits, churches, or other organizations. To improve place strategies, campaigns should "be there at the point of decision making," as much as possible (Lee & Kotler, 2011, p. 295). Our focus-group participants suggested community clinics and pharmacies as appropriate locations for communicating about SP. Indeed, many immigrants remember receiving medical advice from the *boticario* ("apothecary"). Identifying pharmacists as medical providers is reinforced by how pharmacists in Mexico provide services that only a doctor can in the US (e.g., directly dispensing certain antibiotics without a prescription).

Focus-group participants identified one geographical problem: moving around or relocating can jeopardize one's status with SP. To further ease access to SP, marketing efforts could communicate the *permanency* of one's eligibility and ability to use SP to overcome this objection. The ability to update one's address should be made easy, since a fundamental tenet of behavior-change theories is that "the person perceives that he or she has the capabilities to perform the behavior under a number of different circumstances" (Lee & Kotler, 2011, p. 201). Another geographical objection of focus-group participants was that it didn't seem realistic to receive health care while only in Mexico for, say, two weeks during visits to see family. Barriers like this must be addressed to effectively reach audiences. If a host of conditions can be treated quickly by immigrants during short visits, this should be alluded to in advertising in the NY area. It would also be possible for immigrants who return regularly to Mexico to get routine health care there. We might, in such an ad, contrast the frantic pace of life in NY with the more leisurely pace while visiting friends in Mexico, and recommend visiting *tu amigo, el doctor local en la clínica en tu pueblo* ("your friend, the local doctor in the clinic in your town").

To Reduce Barriers to Programs like SP, Move from Cost-Benefit Promotions to Identity-Based Social Marketing

SP and similar programs could use more specific identity appeals in their communications. To create persuasive messages, we needed to learn what kind of identities our participants would take pride in: naming priority audiences isn't a neutral process. Indeed, over five decades of research supports this strategy (Cialdini, 2008; Freedman & Fraser, 1966). March (1994) calls this a move from a "consequences" to an "identity" model of influence: rather than motivating audiences by outlining costs/benefits, we should first appeal to who they think they are. Our focus-group results identified audiences for SP's communication efforts, including "Mexicans in New York," *personas de escasos recursos* (referring partly to themselves and to family members in Mexico), and "Mexicans in New York who may return to Mexico for vacation or to visit family."

In social marketing terms, a priority audience member should perceive "that performance of the behavior is more consistent than inconsistent with his or her self-image, or that its performance does not violate personal standards that activate negative self-actions" (Lee & Kotler, 2019, p. 103). Although the group that would be numerically smallest would be those with chronic conditions or serious illnesses, they would be most inclined to act. For marketing purposes, it's important to "start with target audiences most ready for action" (Lee & Kotler, 2011, p. 59). Accordingly, weighting audiences from most to least important is critical to communication efforts. For SP, the following scheme would assist in the development of segmenting and prioritizing audiences for messages: immigrants likely to return for illness, Mexican immigrants in NY, Mexicans who might visit Mexico, and then others, such as *jefeljefa de familia* ("head of the family").

The "Don't Mess with Texas" antilittering campaign is a classic example of how the public often cannot be motivated to change or modify a behavior until their very identities become part of a campaign—in this case, the perception that Texans are the kind of people who take pride in not littering (Heath & Heath, 2007, pp. 182–199). Many other public-sector "pride" campaigns have demonstrated the power of this communication strategy, in which advocates "grow the[ir] people," as in efforts to instill in nurses that their profession is a kind of calling, and the "Rare" environmental conservation project (www.rareconservation.org) to save the Saint Lucia Parrot (Heath & Heath, 2010, p. 152).

Focus-group participants thought that Mexicans should know they have a "right" to use SP. While we tested other language, such as whether participants thought that descriptors such as "head of household" and many other terms would most appeal to them, we found that primarily *Mexicans en Nueva York* and secondarily concepts like *bajos, pocos o escasos recursos* ("low or few resources") found the most resonance, as well as Mexicans who may visit Mexico on vacation and to visit family, or Mexicans with illnesses who may return. In the "about" section of the SP Facebook page that we examined, eligible program users were first described as "lawyers, architects, and engineers." This is an example of how identity marketing might be leveraged. These descriptions should be updated to fit with the audiences most likely to subscribe to SP, and include fitting descriptors for transnational Mexican audiences with job categories not currently used, such as street vendors and day laborers.

One final comment is worth underscoring. SP videos need to rethink how they show SP users. Our research supported the idea that people used in any commercials should be selected strategically *and* real (i.e., *not* actors). These people could be from a variety of circumstances and professions but could mostly be young immigrants and parents, since Mayra and Humberto appeared to inspire more confidence in our video showings and also focused on providing "family" coverage above and beyond other messaging.

Focus on Returnees and the Otros Dreamers, Who Can Be Enrolled in and Helped by Seguro Popular

This recommendation is first an endorsement of SP's efforts to date to reach out to *retornados* but, in line with our previous four recommendations, also an encouragement to do far more. To reiterate, there are more than a half-million US-raised Mexican youth who have been deported to Mexico and another half-million US citizens who have returned to Mexico, either with their deported family members, or when their families returned voluntarily (Anderson & Solis, 2014; Escobar Latapí, Lowell, & Martin, 2013; Zuñiga, 2015; Zuñiga & Hamann, 2008). In 2015, there were 559,416 returned migrants in Mexico, mainly in Jalisco (51,578), Baja California (49,549), Michoacán (42,836), Guanajuato (35,778), and Estado de México (33,593) (Giorguli & León Bautista, 2018). As a group, they're less likely than Mexico-residing Mexicans to know about SP but also especially likely to need such health services (Escobar Latapí et al., 2013). After years of living in the US and avoiding health institutions, except in cases of an emergency, many migrants may have underlying health issues that need attention, or may have been unable to do basic maintenance for their health, such as going to the dentist or for regular medical checkups. Some have more serious health needs and might experience social vulnerability in the US and Mexico. SP is a good first approach to these issues for this population. *Retornados* are often disoriented and risk extreme marginalization, partly because many have little family in Mexico (their families are in the US), and hence they're deposited where they know no one, don't know the culture, may not speak the language, and have no networks. It's a recipe for suffering.

SP and the Mexican government have taken important steps toward enrolling *retornados* in health care and other programs, although more needs to be done. SP officials have partnered with state and local officials to increase enrollments among returned migrants in border and non-border states such as Coahuila, Nuevo León, and San Luis Potosí. In 2007, the Mexican government began a Repatriation Program in which the Health Ministry offers enrollment in SP to *retornados* at the border (INM, 2017). In a separate study, Escobar Latapí et al. (2013) found that rates of enrollment in SP increased for internal migrants (e.g., intra-Mexico migration), from 2.5% in 2005 to 11.9% in 2010, and for Mexican returned migrants (e.g., international migrants from Mexico who were living in the US), from 5.5% to 22% in the same period. (These *retornados* could have enrolled prior to migrating or upon return.) SP is the most common access to health care among current *retornados*. In a recent survey conducted by the Colegio de la Frontera Norte (www.colef.mx/emif), 37% of *retornados* reported being enrolled in SP (most prior to their emigration from Mexico), compared with only 6% in IMSS and less than 1% in ISSSTE, Mexico's other major public health policies and programs. We were delighted to learn that a "Seguro Popular app" was introduced in 2017, although there are no data yet on its use. After December 2018, prominent changes to SP are expected under AMLO's presidency.

SP and the Mexican government have recognized the needs of other kinds of migrants, including Mexican women migrating within Mexico, and Central American refugees and transmigrants from other countries within Mexico. Empirical evidence shows that refugees have a health disadvantage compared with the rest of the immigrant population in the US (Reed & Yrizar Barbosa, 2017). In 2009, the Mexican federal government agreed to provide SP coverage to international refugees and their families. The National Health Ministry promoted (via *Oficio 326*), among the Subnational Health Ministries in Mexico, health services to all female migrant workers, regardless of nationality or legal status (SRE, 2011b). More needs to be done, according to civil organizations working with migrants. The Institute for Women in Migration (IMUMI, for its Spanish acronym) notes that the Special Migration Program (Programa Especial de Migración), 2014–2018— the main (and most recent and comprehensive) federal policy by the Mexican state on migratory issues—lacks resources to fully implement its programs for migrant women (IMUMI, 2016).

Concerns about *retornado* access to health care remain. While noting the positive growth in the percentage of *retornados* enrolled in SP, Escobar Latapí et al. (2013) argue, echoing our findings reported above, that this enrollment frequently offers thin or patchy coverage. The "paper" coverage, the percentage of people enrolled, is greater than the actual percentage of people getting access to good health care. Moreover, there is a missed opportunity for Mexico to promote the use of SP among potential *retornados*. The Colegio de la Frontera Norte EMIF survey cited above reports that less than 5% of these *retornados* knew about the Health Windows program (consular-based programs promoting access to health knowledge and care in the US) or the Vete Sano, Regresa Sano program, which seeks to ensure that migrants have access to health care before migrating and when returning. This could be done by expanding SP's reach via the Ministry of Foreign Affairs, by strengthening the Consular Protection and Assistance Program (Programa de Protección y Asistencia Consular) regarding the repatriation of *retornado* patients (*repatriación de pacientes*)—i.e., of Mexicans residing abroad who need additional health attention or treatment in Mexico (SRE, 2015). According to Paris Pombo (2010), the Mexican state's response to the needs created by the processes of repatriation was weak compared with the response by civil society, especially considering the role that 19 migrant shelters[4] played at the northern border area of Mexico in 2004–2009 in promoting their human rights and providing services. A comprehensive evaluation of the Instituto Nacional de Migración (National Institute of Migration) in Mexico, which controls and monitors migration flows at the federal level, notes that the budget for the Programa de Repatriación Humana (Humane Repatriation Program) is insufficient for the volume of people returned to Mexico (Insyde, 2013).

Mexico will likely face high levels of *retornados*, transmigrants, and refugees in the medium-term future, and at least until the 2020 US elections. President Bush deported some two million people in his two terms as president; President Obama deported more than 2.8 million during 2009–2015—earning him the moniker "Deporter in Chief" from immigrants-rights advocates, a label that reportedly spurred him to act by creating DACA. Yet in his second administration, Obama pivoted to focus more on deporting criminal aliens, and directed immigration enforcement to try to avoid "sensitive areas" like churches, schools, or courts. DACA was a temporary measure to help Dreamers until Congress acted to fix the problem permanently, by creating a road to legal status. This is unlikely now. Donald Trump made anti-immigrant rhetoric—specifically, an anti-Mexican rhetoric focusing predominantly on undocumented Mexican immigrants who commit crimes—a central plank in his campaign and of his administration to this point. How many deportations his administration will conduct is unknown, but some researchers anticipate the return of at least three million old and sick migrants to Mexico in the next ten years (García Zamora, 2017; Huerta, 2015). Indeed, the government of the City of Mexico reports that it helped more than 20,000 *retornados* in the first six months of 2017 (Romero Sanchez, 2017). During January–March 2017, more than 13,000 people deported from the US were enrolled in SP at 11 points of entry in Mexican border states (Suman, 2017). Trump's public statements indicate that he plans to deport up to some two million current immigrants. Thus far, his administration has changed US policy, using small infractions, such as a past conviction for driving under the influence, as a reason to deport people, including many who have US-citizen children (Chisti & Mittelstadt, 2016).

SP and similar programs could communicate much more effectively with immigrants by aligning applied research, established theories, and on-the-ground developments to form campaigns that are measurable and distinct in their outreach. Truly listening to immigrants rather than broadcasting information at them should be the most critical consideration for any project that hopes to work better with transnational communities. In this spirit, Atkin & Freimuth (2013) urge research and campaign designers to remain flexible and open to what audiences have to say:

> Using a research-based approach [to communication and marketing] in the public service domain is challenging when the mind-set of personnel in sponsoring organizations entails rigid advocacy of unpalatable, ideal behavior … and self-indulgent artistic expression. Furthermore, specialists in domains such as health, environment, or altruism aren't always conscious of the fact that they differ substantially from their audiences in topical knowledge, values, priorities, and level of involvement.
>
> (p. 53)

Whether immigration, health care, education, or one of the many other pressing issues in public affairs, our biggest goal should be, as Dervin and Foreman-Wernet (2013) put it, "to build and sustain genuinely and iteratively responsive communication systems" (p. 160). We advocate that governments, local bureaucracies, and other organizations should aim higher, crafting stronger engagements with immigrant communities within the US and across the world.

In closing, we reiterate our support for the premise behind the Seguro Popular study, which recognizes that Mexicans in the US and in Mexico are often members of transnational families and communities, and may live that way for many years, even a generation or more. SP and CIDE commissioned the study to promote the use of a valuable program by the migrant community and their families, who, they suspected, were largely not using it. Not discounting the political mileage the administration hoped to get, the effort was laudable and is actionable going forward. The insights regarding how to communicate with migrants so that they will listen to and act on the invitation to use the program should be of interest to Mexico and other sending countries, as well as to the US and other destination countries. Understanding how to use social marketing will become increasingly important in the coming years, as the US and other destination countries work across borders and boundaries to integrate many immigrants and their children into their societies.

Notes

1 In the social marketing literature, this core part of a campaign is referred to as monetary costs or burdens dealing with perceived "price."
2 In places like Puebla, this hasn't happened for a variety of reasons. In some cases, political or civil society organizations have organized beyond the local *municipio* level, although this is less common.
3 An important update on access to SP: by January 2019, SP was offering a website to locate affiliation centers (or *Módulos de Afiliación y Orientación*: www.cnpss-dgao.gob.mx/georeferenciadgao/). E.g., in the municipality of Matehuala (pop. 99,015 in 2015, according to INEGI), in the state of San Luis Potosí, there were two affiliation centers out of 64 affiliation centers in the state. However, in Terrenate (pop. 14,746 in 2015), in Tlaxcala, there were no affiliation centers. SP's website provided information for 1,716 affiliation centers in the 32 states in Mexico. The location function was also available in the SP app, offering addresses as well as days and hours of service in these centers.
4 Centers of support for migrants created and run by civil society, including religious orders, especially the Scalabrinians, a Catholic order of priests who have historically tended to the needs of migrants.

Appendix A

General Characteristics of the SegPop1 and SegPop2 Research Projects

	SegPop1	SegPop2
Final title of the report	*"Estudio del nivel de información sobre el Seguro Popular con que cuenta la Población Migrante Mexicana de la Ciudad de Nueva York, EE.UU."*	"How to Talk to Mexicans in New York about El Seguro Popular"
Main objective	To verify if Mexican immigrants in the United States knew about El Seguro Popular and what services it offered, and if a better strategy might improve the knowledge of this program among Mexican communities in the US	To understand more deeply how Mexican immigrants and community leaders understand and misunderstand SP and to develop approaches and language for disseminating persuasive, actionable information about the program
Time frame for the research/ fieldwork	Summer and fall 2011	Spring and summer 2012
Methodology	Surveys and interviews (849 people participated in the surveys)	Focus groups and interviews in the Mexican Consulate and three NGOs in the Bronx, Staten Island, and Brooklyn (eight focus groups were conducted, with an average participation of five individuals from different social backgrounds)

(Continued)

	SegPop1	*SegPop2*
Population/ Subjects studied	Mexican immigrants living in New York City—mainly those who attended the Mexican Consulate in NYC	Mexican immigrants living in New York City—mainly those with a link to a social organization in four of the five NYC boroughs

Appendix B
Seguro Popular in New York Survey

Prof. Robert Courtney Smith

Director del Estudio / Principal Investigator

¿Seguimiento?/Follow up?   Yes/No

Septiembre–Octubre/
September–October 2011

¿Preguntó por afiliarse al SP?/   Yes/No
Asked to enroll in SP?

Fecha /Date: _____

Nombre del encuestador /
Name of the interviewer: _____

Lugar / Place: _____

Buenas Tardes/Días: Estamos haciendo un estudio para ver cuánto saben los migrantes mexicanos acerca del programa de Seguro Popular en México, por medio del cual todo los mexicanos que viven en México pueden tener acceso a un seguro de gastos médicos si no cuentan con otra manera de asegurarse, por ejemplo a través del IMSS, el ISSSTE o un seguro privado. Good Afternoon/Good Day. We are doing a study to see how much Mexican migrants know about the Seguro Popular Program in Mexico, through which all Mexicans who live in Mexico can get access to health insurance for medical expenditures, if they do not have other health insurance, for example, via IMSS, el ISSSTE or private insurance.

- El Seguro Popular puede cubrir a los familiares de los migrantes que viven en México.

  Seguro Popular can cover the migrants' family members who live in Mexico.

- Nos gustaría hacerle unas preguntas sobre este tema del Seguro Popular y al terminar le proporcionaremos información sobre este programa, incluyendo una página de Internet para buscar más datos.

We would like to ask some questions about Seguro Popular, and when we finish that we can give you information about the program, including an Internet page to find more information.

• La encuesta puede ser anónima si usted quiere. Es decir, no es obligatorio que nos proporcione su nombre.

The survey can be anonymous if you like. That is to say, it is not mandatory that you give us your name.

• Es una encuesta voluntaria, por lo que puede decidir no contestar o dejar de contestar en cualquier momento que usted quiera.

It is a voluntary survey, and hence you can decide not to answer or stop answering any questions at any time you like.

• Esta información será utilizada exclusivamente para mejorar el Seguro Popular.

This information will be used exclusively to make Seguro Popular better.

• La encuesta no la hace el gobierno sino la Universidad de la Ciudad de Nueva York (Baruch College, CUNY).

The survey is not being done by the government, but rather by the City University of New York, Baruch College, CUNY.

1. DATOS PERSONALES/PERSONAL INFORMATION
1) Sexo/Sex: Hombre/Man   Mujer/Woman
2) ¿En qué año nació?/What year were you born?
3) ¿Dónde nació?/Where were you born?   Estado/State   Municipio/Town
4) ¿Cuánto tiempo lleva viviendo en Estados Unidos?/How much time have you lived in the US?
5) ¿Aparte de NY, dónde más ha vivido?/Apart from NY, where else have you lived?
6) ¿Hasta qué año llegó en la escuela?/Up to what year in school did you go?
7) ¿A qué se dedica?/What is your work?
8) ¿Cuál es su código postal aquí en NY?/What is your NY zip code?
9) ¿Cuál es la estación de *subway* (o metro) más cercana a su domicilio?/What is the closest subway station to where you live?
10) ¿Habla una lengua indígena? ¿Cuál?/Do you speak an indigenous language? Which one?

2. SALUD Y COBERTURA MÉDICA/HEALTH AND MEDICAL COVERAGE

[a]13) ¿Qué tipo de cobertura médica tiene usted aquí en Estados Unidos?/What type of medical coverage do you have in the United States?

1	2	3	4	5	6	7	8
No tengo/ I don't have	Por medio de mi trabajo/ Through my work	Por medio de un sindicato/ Through a union	Por medio de mi esposa(o)/ un familiar/ Through my wife, husband or relative	Programas públicos/ Public programs	Seguro privado/ Private insurance	Opciones/ Options HHC	Otro/Other: _____

14) Si tiene hijos/as, ¿qué cobertura tienen ellos/as?/If you have children, what coverage do they have?

1	2	3	4	5	6	7	8
No tengo/ I don't have	Por medio de mi trabajo/ Through my work	Por medio de un sindicato/ Through a union	Por medio de mi esposa(o)/ un familiar/ Through my wife, husband or relative	Programas públicos/ Public programs	Seguro privado/ Private insurance	Opciones/ Options HHC	Otro/Other: _____

Space for the interviewer to write out if they have a story (e.g., some of my kids have coverage, some don't)

What particular program are they using?

a Note: The numbering goes from question 10 to question 13 because we had to reconcile different versions of the survey and we developed it. Leaving out numbers 11 and 12 on another survey helped make the data reconcilable. It is not a typo.

15) ¿En los últimos dos años, ha tenido problemas de salud? / In the last two years, have you had any health problems?

Sí   No

----------> **IF NO TO #15, GO TO #17** <----------

16) ¿Ha buscado atención médica?/Have you sought medical care?

Sí   No

17) ¿En los últimos dos años, cuántas veces visito usted al doctor?/ How many times have you gone to the doctor in the last two years?

18) ¿Que obstáculos ha encontrado o considera que puede encontrar al buscar atención médica?/ What obstacles have you faced or think you will face in seeking medical attention?

1	2	3	4	5	6
No tengo seguro/I don't have insurance	Costo/Cost	Muy ocupado con el trabajo/Very busy with work	Porque no tengo papeles/Because I don't have papers	No sé dónde buscar ayuda médica/I don't know where to seek medical help/attention	Otros factores/ Other factors: _____

19) ¿En los últimos dos años, algún miembro de su familia se ha enfermado ya sea aquí o en México?/ In the last two years, has any member of your family been sick here or in Mexico?

Sí   No

3. SEGURO POPULAR

20) ¿Sabía usted que puede tener acceso al seguro médico para usted y su familia por medio del SP?/
Did you know that you and your family can get access to medical insurance and treatment through Seguro Popular?

1	2	3
No sabía nada sobre el programa/I did not know anything at all about the program	He escuchado del programa pero no conozco los detalles/I had heard about the program but did not know the details	Conozco este programa en detalle/ I knew about this program and its details

21) ¿Usted conoce cuáles son los requisitos para calificar para el SP?/
Are you aware under what terms you can qualify for SP?

         Si   No

Les puede decir, DESPUÉS DE ESTA PREGUNTA, que una condición es no tener otro sistema de seguro social (IMSS, ISSSTE…) /
You can tell them, AFTER THIS QUESTIONS, that one condition is not having any other healthcare system (IMSS, ISSSTE…)

- If they say they have someone there, ask them:
- If they want us to follow up with them in, say, two weeks to ensure that their person in Mexico was able to enroll.
- You can tell them that they can call us and we will talk to the SP people because they want to know what is working.
- Get their number if they want us to follow up: _____
- Write FOLLOW UP in bold CAPS on the front of the survey.
- EACH surveyor will, ideally, do the follow ups of the person they took the info on.

-------------------> **IF NO KNOWLEDGE, EXPLAIN IT AND GO TO #23** <-------------------

22) ¿Usted tiene familiares que podrían ser elegibles para el Seguro Popular? /
Do you have family who you think would be eligible for this coverage in Mexico?

         Si   No

-------------------> **IF NO KNOWLEDGE, EXPLAIN IT AND GO TO #28** <-------------------

23) ¿Después de esta explicación, considera que algún familiar califica para el Seguro Popular?/
After this explanation, do you think you have a family member who qualifies for SP?

1 Esposa/o/ Wife/Husband	2 Padre/Madre/ Father/Mother	3 Abuelitos/as/ Grandparents	4 Otros /Others: _____

24) ¿Ha hablado usted con algún familiar en México sobre este programa? /
Have you talked to a family member in Mexico about this program?

Sí   No

25) Si contestó que "sí" a la pregunta #24: ¿Han usado esta cobertura médica sus familiares? /
If you answered yes to question #24: Has your family member used this medical coverage?

Sí   No

26) ¿De qué manera lo han usado, o por qué no lo han usado? / In what way have you used it, or why have not you used it?
Note: write down responses (code after)

27) ¿Cómo se enteró usted de este programa? Marcar todos los que apliquen. How have you learned of these programs?
Check all that apply.

1 Radio	2 Television	3 Internet	4 Periódico Newspaper	5 Amigos o familia *friends or family*	6 Organizaciones comunitarias *community organizations*	7 Consulado Mexicano *Mexican Consulate*	8 Por medio del encuestador *through the surveyor*	9 Otro Other: _____

4. PREGUNTAS DE DIÁSPORA / DIASPORA QUESTIONS

28) Por favor indique que tanto está de acuerdo con la siguiente oración / Please indicate how much you agree with the following sentence:

México se preocupa por el bienestar de sus migrantes en los EU. / Mexico is concerned with the welfare of its migrants in the US.

1	2	3	4	5
Muy en desacuerdo / Strongly disagree	En desacuerdo / Disagree	Indiferente / Indifferent	De acuerdo / Agree	Muy de acuerdo / Strongly agree

29) ¿Que opinión cree que tienen los mexicanos sobre las personas que emigran a E.U.? / What do you think Mexicans think of people who have emigrated to the US?

1	2	3
Negativo	Indiferente	Positivo

30) ¿Ha regresado usted a México desde que vive en EU? Have you returned to Mexico since you have lived in the US?

Sí	No

31) ¿Si contesta que sí, ¿cuántas veces ha ido a México? If they answer yes, how many times have you gone to Mexico?

32) Usted es / You are:

1	2	3	4	5	6
Ciudadano Americano / US citizen	Residente permanente (Green Card)/ Permanent resident	Tengo visa / Visa holder	Indocumentado / Undocumented	Prefiere no contester / I prefer not to answer	Visa vencida / Expired visa (Overstayed)

5. OTHER

33) ¿Le interesaría recibir más información sobre el Seguro Popular?
Would you be interested in receiving more information about the Seguro Popular program?   Sí   No

-------------------> **Ask if they want us to send them a packet** <-------------------

34) Si fuera posible, ¿le interesaría recibir atención médica del SP en E.U.? /
If it were possible, would you be interested in getting medical care from Seguro Popular in the US?   Sí   No

Write down story or comments on it:

35) Nos gustaría invitarlo a participar en una entrevista más extensa sobre el tema. ¿Le interesaría participar? /
Would you be interested in doing a longer interview about your experiences?   Sí   No

36) Si bien no es obligatorio, ¿le importaría darme sus datos personales? / While it is not mandatory, would you like to give me your contact information?

If yes, please give me your contact info:

Teléfono / Phone: Correo electrónico / Email:
Dirección / Address: Ciudad / City:
Estado / State: Código postal / Zip code:

37) ¿Tiene algún otro comentario que le gustaría hacer? / Is there any other comment you would like to make?

GRACIAS POR SU APOYO PARA REALIZAR ESTA ENCUESTA. /
Thank you for your support in doing this survey.

TODA LA INFORMACIÓN QUE USTED NOS HA DADO ES ESTRICTAMENTE CONFIDENCIAL. /
All the information you have given us is strictly confidential.

PARA MÁS INFORMACIÓN: /
For more information:
: www.seguropopular.gob.mx[b]

---

b Note: Link no longer available.

References

Aaker, J., & Smith, A. (2010). *The dragonfly effect: Quick, effective, and powerful ways to use social media to drive social change.* San Francisco, CA: Jossey-Bass.

Abbott, A. (2001). *Time matters.* Chicago, IL: University of Chicago Press.

Alanís Enciso, F. S., & Alarcón Acosta, R. (Eds.). (2016). *El ir y venir de los norteños: Historia de la migración mexicana a Estados Unidos (Siglos XIX–XXI).* Mexico: Colegio de la Frontera Norte/Colegio de San Luis/Colegio de Michoacán.

Alarcón, R. (2006). Hacia la construcción de una política de emigración en México. In C. González Gutiérrez (Ed.), *Relaciones estado–diáspora: Aproximaciones desde cuatro continentes* (Vol. 1, pp. 157–179). Mexico: Miguel Ángel Porrúa, UAZ, SRE, IME, ANUIES.

Alarcón, R., & Yrizar Barbosa, G. (2015). The threat of deportation among undocumented parents with US citizen children in Los Angeles. Unpublished manuscript.

Alatorre, A. (2016, June 6). Desvían recursos del Seguro Popular. *Reforma.* www.reforma.com/aplicaciones/articulo/default.aspx?id=785484

Alba, R., & Yrizar Barbosa, G. (2016). Room at the top? Minority mobility and the transition to demographic diversity in the USA. *Ethnic and Racial Studies, 39,* 917–938.

Anderson, J. (2015). Tagged as a criminal: Narratives of deportation and return migration in a Mexico City call center. *Latino Studies, 13,* 8–27.

Anderson, J., & Solis, N. (2014). *Los otros dreamers.* Iniciativa Ciudadana A.C. México: U.S.–Mexico Foundation.

Andreasen, A. (2005). *Social marketing in the 21st century.* Thousand Oaks, CA: Sage Publications.

Andresen, K. (2006). *Robin Hood marketing: Stealing corporate savvy to sell just causes.* San Francisco, CA: Jossey-Bass.

Arenas, E., Goldman, N., Pebley, A. R., & Teruel, G. (2015). Return migration to Mexico: Does health matter? *Demography, 52,* 1853–1868.

Asamani-Asante, N. O. (2014). *Predictors of West African immigrants' satisfaction with healthcare providers: Self-efficacy, stages of change, and skill for navigating service delivery in the United States* (Doctoral dissertation). Teachers College, Columbia University.

Asgedom, M. G. (2015). *The experience of Eritrean immigrants regarding utilisation of healthcare services in Indianapolis, Indiana, USA* (Master's thesis). University of South Africa.

Asis, M. M. B., & Baggio, F. (2008). Will turning transnational foster development in the Philippines? In M. M. B. Asis & F. Baggio (Eds.), *Moving out, back and up: International migration and development prospects in the Philippines* (pp. 1–16). Philippines: Scalabrini Migration Center.

Atkin, C. K., & Freimuth, V. (2013). Guidelines for formative evaluation research in campaign design. In R. E. Rice & C. K. Atkin (Eds.), *Public communication campaigns* (4th ed., pp. 53–68). Thousand Oaks, CA: Sage Publications.

Bada, X., & Gleeson, S. (2015). A new approach to migrant labor rights enforcement: The crisis of undocumented worker abuse and Mexican consular advocacy in the United States. *Labor Studies Journal, 40*, 32–53.

Bader, A., Musshauser, D., Sahin, F., Bezirkan, H., & Hochleitner, M. (2006). The mosque campaign: A cardiovascular prevention program for female Turkish immigrants. *Wiener Klinische Wochenschrift, 118*, 217–223.

Banning, M. (2008). A review of clinical decision making: Models and current research. *Journal of Clinical Nursing, 17*, 187–195.

Baranowski, T., Buday, R., Thompson, D. I., & Baranowski, J. (2008). Playing for real: Video games and stories for health-related behavior change. *American Journal of Preventive Medicine, 34*, 74–82.

Barba Solano, C. (2010). La reforma de la ley General de Salud en México y la creación del Seguro Popular: ¿Hacia la cobertura universal? In V. Lomelí (Ed.), *Perspectivas del universalismo en México* (pp. 87–102). México: ITESO/Universidad de Guadalajara/Konrad Adenauer Stiftung/ Universidad Iberoamericana.

Barnett, J. (2011, October 4). Writing effective Facebook posts. *Social Media Today*. http://socialmediatoday.com/bigsea/370308/writing-effective-facebook-posts

Baron, J. (2004). Normative models of judgement and decision making. In D. J. Koehler & N. Harvey (Eds.), *Blackwell handbook of judgement and decision making* (pp. 19–36). London: Blackwell.

Barrios-Paoli, L. (2015). Improving immigrant access to health care in New York City: A report from the Mayor's Task Force on immigrant health-care access. NYC.gov. www1.nyc.gov/assets/home/downloads/pdf/reports/2015/ immigrant-health-task-force-report.pdf

Bauböck, R., & Faist, T. (Eds.). (2010). *Diaspora and transnationalism: Concepts, theories, and methods.* Amsterdam: IMISCOE Research, University of Amsterdam Press.

Bauböck, R. (2007). Stakeholder citizenship and transnational political participation: A normative evaluation of external voting. *Fordham Law Review, 75*, 2393–2447.

Bergad, L. (2013). Demographic, economic and social transformations in the Mexican-origin population of the New York City metropolitan area, 1990–2010. Latino Data Report #49. Center for Latin American, Caribbean and Latino Studies, City University of New York, New York.

Besserer, F. (2004). *Topografías transnacionales: Hacia una geografía de la vida transnacional.* México DF: Universidad Autónoma Metropolitana.

Blanding, M. (2014, July 16). Marketing Obamacare. *Harvard Business School working knowledge.* http://hbswk.hbs.edu/item/7566.html

Bleich, S., Cutler, D., Adams, A., Lozano, R., & Murray, C. (2007). Impact of insurance and supply of health professionals on coverage of treatment for hypertension in Mexican population-based study. *British Medical Journal, 335,* 875.

Border Health Commission (BHS) or Comisión Nacional Fronteriza (CSF). (2011, April 4). Colaboración binacional y vigilancia de enfermedades infecciosas a lo largo de la frontera México–Estados Unidos: Informe. www.borderhealth.org/files/res_1879.pdf

Boyce, M. E. (1995). Collective centering and collective sense-making in the stories and story-telling of one organization. *Organization Studies, 16,* 107–137.

Brady, H. (2005). Data-set observations versus causal-process observations: The 2000 U.S. presidential election. In H. Brady & D. Collier (Eds.), *Rethinking social inquiry: Diverse tools, shared standards* (pp. 237–242). Lanham, MD: Rowman & Littlefield.

Brand, L. (2006). Marruecos: La evolución de la participación institucional del estado en las comunidades diáspora. In C. González Gutiérrez (Ed.), *Relaciones estado–diáspora: Aproximaciones desde cuatro continentes* (Vol. 1, pp. 99–136). México: Miguel Ángel Porrúa, UAZ, SRE, IME, ANUIES.

Buller, D. B., Walkosz, B. J., Andersen, P. A., Scott, M. D., Dignan, M. B., & Cutter, G. R. (2013). The go sun smart campaign: Achieving individual and organizational change for occupational sun protection. In R. E. Rice & C. K. Atkin (Eds.), *Public communication campaigns* (4th ed., pp. 191–204). Thousand Oaks, CA: Sage Publications.

Carrasco-Garrido, P., Jiménez-García, R., Barrera, V. H., de Andrés, A. L., & de Miguel, Á. G. (2009). Significant differences in the use of healthcare resources of native-born and foreign-born in Spain. *BMC Public Health, 9,* 201.

Cheney, G., Christensen, L. T., Zorn, T. E., Jr., & Ganesh, S. (2011). *Organizational communication in an age of globalization: Issues, reflections, practices.* Long Grove, IL: Waveland Press.

Cheng, H., Kotler, P., & Lee, N. (2009). *Social marketing for public health: Global trends and success stories.* Sudbury, MA: Jones and Bartlett.

Chisti, M., & Mittelstadt, M. (2016). Unauthorized immigrants with criminal convictions: Who might be a priority for removal. Migration Policy Institute. www.migrationpolicy.org/news/unauthorized-immigrants-criminal-convictions-who-might-be-priority-removal

Choate, M. (2009). *Emigrant nation: The making of Italy abroad.* Cambridge, MA: Harvard University Press.

Christiano, A., & Neimand, A. (2017). Stop raising awareness already. *Stanford Social Innovation Review*. https://ssir.org/articles/entry/stop_raising_ awareness_already

Cialdini, R. (2008). *Influence: Science and practice* (5th ed.). New York, NY: Allyn & Bacon.

Colarossi, L. G., Hazel, D. S., Collier, K. L., DeSouza, S., & Pappas, L. (2016). Research with Latina and Black women for an HIV prevention campaign. *Social Marketing Quarterly, 22*, 1–17.

Collyer, M. (Ed.). (2013). *Emigration nations: Policies and ideologies of emigrant engagement*. New York, NY: Palgrave Macmillan.

Cordasco, E. (1980). *Italian mass emigration*. Totowa, NJ: Rowman & Littlefield.

Córdova Villalobos, J. A. (2010, November 22). Universal health coverage: The Mexican case. Presentation to the German Federal Ministry of Health, Berlin. http://www.bmg.bund.de/fileadmin/redaktion/pdf_who/Presentation_ Mexico_Berlin_22_Nov_2010.pdf

Cousineau, M., Stevens, G., & Farias, A. (2010). Measuring the impact of outreach and enrollment strategies for public health insurance in California. *Health Services Research, 46*, 319–335.

Davis, R. (2012a). Social media that works. *Blue State Digital*. http://www. bluestatedigital.com/page/signup/bsd-webinar-social-media

Davis, R. (2012b, June). *Blue State Digital*. Seminar at Baruch College. New York, NY.

Délano, A. (2010). *Diagnóstico del Instituto de los Mexicanos en el Exterior*. México: Banco Interamericano de Desarrollo/Fundación para la Productividad en el Campo.

Délano, A. (2011). *Mexico and its diaspora in the United States: Policies of emigration since 1848*. New York, NY: Cambridge University Press.

Délano, A. (2014). The diffusion of diaspora engagement policies: A Latin America agenda. *Political Geography, 41*, 90–100.

Délano. A. (2018). *A bridge to membership: Diaspora policies, integration and precarious status migrants in North America*. New York, NY: Oxford University Press.

Délano, A., & Yrizar Barbosa, G. (2017). Políticas hacia los emigrantes en Estados Unidos, de lo nacional a lo estatal: Lecciones del caso de Michoacán. In C. Heller & E. Corral (Eds.), *El impacto sociocultural del fenómeno migratorio en Michoacán* (pp. 343–373). Mexico: Centro de Cooperación Regional para la Educación de Adultos en América Latina y el Caribe (CREFAL).

De la Puente, M. (1993). *Using ethnography to explain why people are missed or erroneously included by the census: Evidence from small area ethnographic studies*. Washington, DC: U.S. Census Bureau.

Dervin, B., & Foreman-Wernet, L. (2013). Sense-making methodology as an approach to understanding and designing for campaign audiences: A turn to communicating communicatively. In R. E. Rice & C. K. Atkin (Eds.), *Public communication campaigns* (4th ed., pp. 147–162). Thousand Oaks, CA: Sage Publications.

Díaz, D., Castañeda Pérez, M. A., & Meneses Navarro, S. (2010). *Implicaciones del Seguro Popular en la reducción de la muerte materna: Perspectiva a nivel nacional y en los estados de Chiapas y Oaxaca.* México: Fundar. https://siid.insp.mx/documentos/curriculo/libros_capitulos/com-1016141238.pdf

Dillard, J. P., Weber, K. M., & Vail, R. G. (2007). The relationship between the perceived and actual effectiveness of persuasive messages: A meta-analysis with implications for formative campaign research. *Journal of Communication, 57*, 613–631.

Dominguez, B., & Mahler, S. J. (1993). Alternative enumeration of undocumented Mexicans in South Bronx. Prepared under Joint Statistical Agreement 89–46 with Columbia University. Washington, DC: Bureau of the Census.

Dorfman, L., & Wallack, L. (2013). Putting policy into health communication: The role of media advocacy. In R. E. Rice & C. K. Atkin (Eds.), *Public communication campaigns* (4th ed., pp. 335–348). Thousand Oaks, CA: Sage Publications.

Dunning, T. (2012). *Natural experiments in social sciences: A design-based approach.* New York, NY: Cambridge University Press.

Entertainment Education. (2012, July 9). U.S. Centers for Disease Control and Prevention. www.cdc.gov/healthcommunication/ToolsTemplates/EntertainmentEd/index.html

Escala Rabadán, L. (Ed.). (2016). *Asociaciones inmigrantes y fronteras internacionales.* México: Colegio de la Frontera Norte/Colegio de San Luis.

Escobar Latapí, A., Lowell, L., & Martín, S. (2013). Diálogo binacional sobre migrantes Mexicanos en Estados Unidos y México. Final report, CIESAS, MacArthur Foundation. http://www.cisan.unam.mx/migracionRetorno/ABRIL%2026-%20INFORME%20FINAL%20dialogo%20binacional%20ESP2.pdf

Ewick, P., & Silbey, S. (1995). Subversive stories and hegemonic tales: Toward a sociology of narrative. *Law and Society Review, 29*, 197–226.

Facebook marketing: What can you learn from consumer behaviour? (2012a, March21). *Kronik Media.* www.kronikmedia.co.uk/blog/facebook-marketing-tips-consumer-behaviour/2779/

Facebook marketing: Top 10 posting tips. (2012b, May 21). *Kronik Media.* www.kronikmedia.co.uk/blog/facebook-marketing-top-posting-tips/3078/

Faist, T. (1995). *Social citizenship for whom? Young Turks in Germany and Mexican Americans in the United States.* Avebury: Aldershot.

Finkelstein, A., with Arrow, K. J., Gruber, J., Newhart, J. P., & Stiglitz, J. (2015). *Moral hazard in health insurance.* New York, NY: Columbia University Press.

Fitzgerald, D. S. (2009). *A nation of emigrants: How Mexico manages its migration.* Berkeley, CA: University of California Press.

Fitzgerald, D. S., & Cook-Martin, D. (2014). *Culling the masses: The democratic origins of racist immigration policy in the Americas.* Cambridge, MA: Harvard University Press.

Five killer strategies to dominate social media's big 3: Facebook, Twitter, & YouTube. (2012). Awareness Social Marketing Software. http://info.aware nessnetworks.com/5-Killer-Strategies-For-The-Big-3.html

Flamand, L., & Moreno Jaimes, C. (2014). *Seguro popular y federalismo en México: Un análisis de política pública.* México: CIDE.

Foerster, R. F. (1919). *The Italian emigration of our times.* Cambridge, MA: Harvard University Press.

Fogg, B. J., & Adler, R. (Eds.). (2009). *Texting 4 Health: A simple, powerful way to improve lives.* Stanford, CA: Captology Media.

Foner, N. (Ed.). (2013). *One out of three: Immigrant New York in the twenty-first century.* New York, NY: Columbia University Press.

Fox, J., & Bada, X. (2008). Migrant organizations and hometown impacts in rural Mexico. *Journal of Agrarian Change, 8,* 435–461.

Fox, J., & Rivera-Salgado, G. (2004). *Indigenous Mexican migrants in the United States.* San Diego, CA: Center for Comparative Immigration Studies, University of California Press.

Freedman, J. L., & Fraser, S. C. (1966). Compliance without pressure: The foot in the door technique. *Journal of Personality and Social Psychology, 4,* 195–203.

French, J., Blair-Stevens, C., McVey, D., & Merritt, R. (2010). *Social marketing and public health: Theory and practice.* Oxford: Oxford University Press.

Frenk, J., Sepúlveda, J., Gómez-Dantés, O., & Knaul, F. (2003). Evidence-based health policy: Three generations of reform in Mexico. *Lancet, 363,* 1667–1671.

Friedman, C. P. (2005). "Smallball" evaluation: A prescription for studying community-based information interventions. *Journal of the Medical Library Association, 93,* S43–S48.

Gabaccia, D. (2000). *Italy's many diasporas.* Seattle, WA: University of Washington Press.

Gambetta, R. (2012). Positive crossroads: Mexican consular assistance and immigrant integration. *City Practice Brief, National League of Cities.* www. nlc.org/Documents/Find%20City%20Solutions/Research%20Innovation/ Immigrant%20Integration/positive-crossroads-mexican-consular-assistance-cpb-mar12.pdf

Gamson, W. A., & Modigliani, A. (1989). Media discourse and public opinion on nuclear power: A constructionist approach. *American Journal of Sociology, 95,* 1–37.

García-Acevedo, M. R. (1996). Return to Aztlán: Mexico's policies toward Chicanos. In D. Maciel & I. D. Ortiz (Eds.), *Chicanas/Chicanos at the crossroads: Social, economic, and political change* (pp. 130–155). Tucson, AZ: University of Arizona Press.

García Zamora, R. (2017). *Retorno de los migrantes Mexicanos de Estados Unidos a Michoacán, Oaxaca, Zacatecas, Puebla, Guerrero, y Chiapas, 2000–2012.* México: Miguel Ángel Porrúa/Universidad Autónoma de Zacatecas.

Garza, B. (2015). Increasing the responsiveness of health services in Mexico's Seguro Popular: Three policy proposals for voice and power. *Health Systems & Reform, 1,* 235–245.

Gass, R. H., & Seiter, J. S. (2011). *Persuasion, social influence, and compliance gaining* (4th ed.). New York, NY: Allyn & Bacon.

Giorguli, S., & León Bautista, A. (2018, June). Radiografía de la migración de retorno 2015. Sistema nacional de información sobre migración de retorno y derechos sociales: Barreras a la integración. Notas para la integración de los retornados no. 1. Colegio de México /CNDH.

Glick-Schiller, N., Basch, L., & Szanton-Blanc, C. (1995). From immigrant to transmigrant: Theorizing transnational migration. *Anthropology Quarterly, 68*, 48–63.

Glynn, C. J., Herbst, S., O'Keefe, G., Shapiro, R. Y., & Lindeman, M. (2004). *Public opinion* (2nd ed.). Boulder, CO: Westview Press.

Goffman, E. (1961). *Asylums: Essays on the social situation of mental patients and other inmates*. Garden City, NY: Anchor.

Goldring, L. 1998. The power of status in transnational social fields. In M. P. Smith & L. Guarnizo (Eds.), *Transnationalism from below* (pp. 165–195). New Brunswick, NJ: Transaction.

González Gutiérrez, C. (1999). Fostering identities: Mexico's relations with its diaspora. *Journal of American History, 86*, 545–567.

González Gutiérrez, C. (Ed.). (2006). *Relaciones estado–diáspora: Aproximaciones desde cuatro continentes*. México: Miguel Ángel Porrúa, UAZ, SRE, IME, ANUIES.

Graham, P. M. (2001). Political incorporation and re-incorporation: Simultaneity in the Dominican migrant experience. In H. Cordero-Guzmán, R. C. Smith, & R. Grosfoguel (Eds.), *Migration, transnationalization, and race in a changing New York* (pp. 87–108). Philadelphia, PA: Temple University Press.

Green, N. L., & Waldinger, R. (2016). *A century of transnationalism: Immigrants and their homeland connections*. Urbana, IL: University of Illinois Press.

Guarnizo, L. E. (1998). The rise of transnational social formations: Mexican and Dominican state responses to transnational migration. *Political power and social theory, 12*, 45–94.

Hajer, M. A. (1995). *The politics of environmental discourse: Ecological modernization and the policy process*. Oxford: Oxford University Press.

Hajer, M., & Laws, D. (2006). Ordering through discourse. In M. Moran, M. Rein, & R. Goodin (Eds.), *The Oxford handbook of public policy* (pp. 251–268). New York, NY: Oxford University Press.

Harvey, P. D. (1999). *Let every child be wanted: How social marketing is revolutionizing contraceptive use around the world*. Westport, CT: Auburn House.

Hastings, G. (2007). *Social marketing: Why should the devil have all the best tunes?* Burlington, MA: Butterworth-Heinemann.

Hayden, C., Waisanen, D., & Osipova, Y. (2013). Facilitating the conversation: The 2012 US presidential election and public diplomacy through social media. *American Behavioral Scientist, 57*, 1623–1642.

Health Initiative of the Americas. (2017). https://hia.berkeley.edu/about-us/

Heath, C., & Heath, D. (2007). *Made to stick: Why some ideas survive and others die*. New York, NY: Random House.

Heath, C., & Heath, D. (2010). *Switch: How to change things when change is hard*. New York, NY: Random House.

Helping life-saving lessons reach marginalized Indian communities. (2012, August 8). Sesameworkshop. www.sesameworkshop.org/our-blog/2012/08/08/helping-life-saving-lessons-reach-marginalized-indian-communities/

Hernández-Torres, J., Avila-Burgos, L., Valencia-Mendoza, A., & Poblano-Verástegui, O. (2008). Seguro Popular's initial evaluation of household catastrophic health spending in Mexico. *Revista de Salud Pública (Bogotá)*, *10*, 18–32.

Herrera, M. G., Moncayo, M. I., & Escobar, G. A. (2012). Perfil migratorio del Ecuador 2011. Organización Internacional para las Migraciones. http://publications.iom.int/bookstore/free/Perfil_Migratorio_del_Ecuador2011.pdf

Hibbard, J. H. (2003). Engaging health-care consumers to improve the quality of care. *Medical Care, 41*, 161–170.

Hornik, R. C. (2013). Why can't we sell human rights like soap? In R. E. Rice & C. K. Atkin (Eds.), *Public communication campaigns* (4th ed., pp. 35–52). Thousand Oaks, CA: Sage Publications.

Huerta, D. M. (2015, February 22). Investigadores alertan: Ola de migrantes agotados volverá en 10 años a México, y no hay qué darles. *HuffPost*. www.huffingtonpost.com/2015/02/22/migrantes-mexico-retorno_n_6730350.html

IME [Instituto de los Mexicanos en el Exterior]. (2016, June 8). SRE y Secretaría de Salud promueven el bienestar e integración de connacionales a través de la salud en Nueva York. Boletín Especial Lazos 1672. www.ime.gob.mx/images/stories/lazos/2016/boletines/1672.htm

IMUMI [Instituto para las Mujeres en la Migración, AC]. (2016). Information from Civil Society Organizations (for LOIPR) to CMW—International Convention on the Protection of the Rights of All Migrant Workers and Members of Their Families. Report to UN, Office of the High Commissioner for Human Rights. http://tbinternet.ohchr.org/Treaties/CMW/Shared%20Documents/MEX/INT_CMW_NGO_MEX_24806_S.doc

INM [Instituto Nacional de Migración] (2017, May 1). Programa de Repatriación. www.gob.mx/inm/acciones-y-programas/programa-de-repatriacion-12469

Insyde [Instituto para la Seguridad y la Democracia]. (2013). Diagnóstico del Instituto Nacional de Migración: Hacia un sistema de rendición de cuentas en pro de los derechos de las personas migrantes en México. http://insyde.org.mx/wp-content/uploads/2014/03/Diagnostico_INM_Insyde_2013_Completo

Irazuzta, I., & Yrizar, G. (2006). Gobernar la migración: consideraciones en torno al Instituto de los Mexicanos en el Exterior. In *La migración en México: ¿Un problema sin solución?* (pp. 176–216). México: Centro de Estudios Sociales y de Opinión Pública, Congreso de la Unión (Colección: Legislando la agenda social).

Iskander, N. (2010). *Creative state: Forty years of migration and development policy in Morocco and Mexico*. Ithaca, NY: Cornell University Press.

Jacobs, R., & Sobieraj, S. (2007). Narrative, public policy, and political legitimacy: Congressional debates about the nonprofit sector, 1894–1969. *Sociological Theory, 25*, 1–25.

Jenkins, H. (2006). *Convergence culture: Where old and new media collide.* New York, NY: New York University Press.

Jones, S. R. G. (1992). Was there a Hawthorne effect? *American Journal of Sociology, 98,* 451–446.

Kammer, A., Niessen, S., Schmid, L., & Schwendener, N. (2016). Finding one's way on the roads to social change: The metamodel of the impact of FOPH communication campaigns. *Social Marketing Quarterly, 22,* 1–18.

Karan, K. (2008). Impact of health communication campaigns on health behaviors in Singapore. *Social Marketing Quarterly, 14,* 85–108.

Kennedy, M. G., O'Leary, A., Beck, V., Pollard, K., & Simpson, P. (2009). The soap opera path to health policy goals. In D. Graber (Ed.), *Media politics* (pp. 343–352). Thousand Oaks, CA: Sage Publications.

Kietzmann, J. H., Silvestre, B. S., McCarthy, I. P., & Pitt, L. F. (2012). Unpacking the social media phenomenon: Towards a research agenda. *Journal of Public Affairs, 12,* 109–119.

King, G. (n.d.). Mexican health-care evaluation. https://gking.harvard.edu/category/research-interests/applications/mexican-health-care-evaluation

King, G., Gakidou, E., Ravishankar, N., Moore, R. T., Lakin, J., Vargas, M., … Hernández Llamas, H. (2007). A "politically robust" experimental design for public policy evaluation, with application to the Mexican Universal Health Insurance Program. *Journal of Policy Analysis and Management, 26,* 479–506.

King, G., Gakidou, E., Imai, K., Lakin, J., Moore, R. T., Nall, C., … Hernández Llamas, H. (2009). Public policy for the poor? A randomised assessment of the Mexican Universal Health Insurance Programme. *Lancet, 373,* 1447–1454.

Knaul, F. M., Bhadelia, A., Atun, R., & Frenk, J. (2015). Achieving effective universal health coverage and diagonal approaches to care for chronic illnesses. *Health Affairs, 34,* 1514–1522.

Knaul, F. M., González-Pier, E., Gómez-Dantés, O., García-Junco, D., Arreola-Ornelas, H., Barraza-Lloréns, M., … Frenk, J. (2012). The quest for universal health coverage: Achieving social protection for all in Mexico. *Lancet, 380,* 1259–1279.

Kotler, P., & Lee, N. (2009). *Up and out of poverty: The social marketing solution.* Upper Saddle River, NJ: Wharton School.

Kramer, S. (2011, April 5). Content marketing: Why video works. V3B Marketing Reimagined. https://v3b.com/2011/04/content-marketing-why-video-works/

Lafleur, J. M. (2011). Why do states enfranchise citizens abroad? Comparative insights from Mexico, Italy, and Belgium. *Global Networks, 11,* 481–501.

Lafleur, J. M. (2012). *Transnational politics and the state: The external voting rights of diasporas.* New York, NY: Routledge.

Lakin, J. M. (2010). The end of insurance? Mexico's Seguro Popular, 2001–2007. *Journal of Health Politics, Policy and Law, 35,* 313–352.

Landa, N. (2014). *In search of belonging: The (in)voluntary return of DREAMers to Mexico* (Master's thesis). University College London.

Lanham, R. A. (2006). *The economics of attention: Style and substance in the age of information.* Chicago, IL: University of Chicago Press.

Laurell, A. C. (2014). *Impacto del Seguro Popular en el sistema de salud Mexicano*. CLACSO Latin American Council of Social Sciences. Buenos Aires, Argentina.

Lavielle, G. (2012). Resultados negativos del Seguro Popular en los Estados: Pesos y contrapesos. México: Fundar. www.fundar.org.mx/mexico/pdf/resultadosnegativos.pdf

Lee, G., & Kwak, Y. H. (2012). An open government maturity model for social media-based public engagement. *Government Information Quarterly*, *29*, 492–503.

Lee, N., & Kotler, P. (2011). *Social marketing: Influencing behaviors for good* (4th ed.). Thousand Oaks, CA: Sage Publications.

Lee, N., & Kotler, P. (2016). *Social marketing: Influencing behaviors for good* (5th ed.). Thousand Oaks, CA: Sage Publications.

Lee, N., & Kotler, P. (2019). *Social marketing: Influencing behaviors for good* (6th ed.). Thousand Oaks, CA: Sage Publications.

Lefebvre, R. C. (2009). Integrating cellphones and mobile technologies into public health practice: A social marketing perspective. *Health Promotion Practice*, *10*, 490–494.

Lefebvre, R. C. (2015, July 1). Concept testing: The most important step for social marketing. On Social Marketing and Social Change. https://shar.es/1tjZxF

Lestage, F. (2012). Entre Mexique et États-Unis: La chaîne entrepreneuriale de la mort des migrants. *Revue Européenne des Migrations Internationales*, *28*, 71–88.

Levitt, P. (2001). *The transnational villagers*. Berkeley, CA: University of California Press.

Llanos-Zavalaga, F., Poppe, P., Tawfik, Y., & Church-Balin, C. (2004). *The role of communication in Peru's fight against tuberculosis*. Baltimore, MD: Johns Hopkins Bloomberg School of Public Health.

Lovejoy, K., & Saxton, G. (2012). Information, community, and action: How nonprofit organizations use social media. *Journal of Computer-Mediated Communication*, *17*, 337–353.

Lovett, J. (2011). *Social media metric secrets*. Indianapolis, IN: Wiley.

Luis Fonsi commercial, St. Jude Children's Research Hospital. (2011, November 11). *YouTube*. www.youtube.com/watch?v=v0uOs4doVsI

Magro, M. J. (2012). A review of social media use in e-government. *Administrative Science*, *2*, 148–161.

Manheim, J. (2011). *Strategy in information and influence campaigns: How policy advocates, social movements, insurgent groups, corporations, governments and others get what they want*. New York, NY: Routledge.

March, J. (1994). *A primer on decision making: How decisions happen*. New York, NY: Free Press.

Marietta, M. (2006). Undocumented immigrants should receive social services. *International Social Science Review*, *81*, 61–66.

Martínez-Wenzl, M. (2013). Bi-national education initiatives: A brief history. In B. Jensen & A. Sawyer (Eds.), *Regarding educación: Mexican-American schooling, immigration, and bi-national improvement* (pp. 279–298). New York, NY: Teachers College, Columbia University.

Massey, D. S., Durand, J., & Malone, N. J. (2002). *Beyond smoke and mirrors: Mexican immigration in an era of economic integration.* New York, NY: Russell Sage Foundation.

McKenzie-Mohr, D., & Smith, W. (2011). *Fostering sustainable behavior: An introduction to community-based social marketing* (3rd ed.). Gabriola Island, BC: New Society.

Miller, M. J. (1981). *Foreign workers in Western Europe: An emerging political force.* New York, NY: Praeger.

Mills, A. J. (2012). Virality in social media: SPIN framework. *Journal of Public Affairs, 12,* 162–169.

Moctezuma, M. (2015). El migrante colectivo transnacional: Senda que avanza y reflexión que se estanca. ResearchGate. www.researchgate.net/publication/228848922_El_Migrante_Colectivo_Transnacional_senda_que_avanza_y_reflexin_que_se_estanca

Moy, B., & Chabner, B. A. (2011). Patient navigator programs, cancer disparities, and the patient protection and Affordable Care Act. *Oncologist, 16,* 926–929.

Nielsen, S. S., Yazici, S., Petersen, S. G., Blaakilde, A. L., & Krasnik, A. (2012). Use of cross-border healthcare services among ethnic Danes, Turkish immigrants and Turkish descendants in Denmark: A combined survey and registry study. *BMC Health Services Research, 12,* 390.

Nigenda, G., Wirtz, V. J., González-Robledo, L. M., & Reich, M. R. (2015). Evaluating the implementation of Mexico's health reform: The case of Seguro Popular. *Health Systems & Reform, 1,* 217–218.

Nothhaft, H. (2016). A framework for strategic communication research: A call for synthesis and consilience. *International Journal of Strategic Communication, 10,* 69–86.

O'Flavahan, L., & Goulet, A. (2012, April). *CDC's guide to writing for social media.* U.S. Centers for Disease Control and Prevention. www.cdc.gov/socialmedia/Tools/guidelines/pdf/GuidetoWritingforSocialMedia.pdf

Okamoto, K. (2009–2010). After the bailout: Regulating systemic moral hazard. *UCLA Law Review, 57,* 183–236.

Olney, C. A. (2005). Using evaluation to adapt health information outreach to the complex environments of community-based organizations. *Journal of the Medical Library Association, 93,* S57–S67.

Oristian, E., Sweeney, P., Puentes, V., Jiménez, J., & Ruiz, M. M. (2009). The migrant health paradox revisited. In W. A. Cornelius, D. Fitzgerald, & S. Borger (Eds.), *Four generations of Norteños: New research from the cradle of Mexican migration* (pp. 217–239). San Diego, CA: Center for Comparative Immigration Studies, University of California Press.

Ottoson, J. M., & Green, L. W. (2005). Community outreach: From measuring the difference to making a difference with health information. *Journal of the Medical Library Association*, *93*, S49–S56.

Overland, S., Glozier, N., Henderson, M., Maeland, J. G., Hotopf, M., & Myketun, A. (2008). Health status before, during and after disability pension award: The Hordaland Health Study. *Occupational and Environmental Medicine*, *65*, 769–773.

Paris Pombo, D. (2010). Procesos de repatriación: Experiencias de las personas devueltas a México por las autoridades Estadounidenses. Woodrow Wilson Center and Colegio de la Frontera Norte. www.wilsoncenter.org/sites/default/files/PARIS%20POMBO%20PAPER.pdf

Park, R. E. (1922). *The immigrant press and its controls*. New York, NY: Harper.

Pease Chock, P. (1995). Ambiguity in policy discourse: Congressional talk about immigration. *Policy Sciences*, *28*, 165–184.

Perrault, E. K., & Silk, K. J. (2014). Testing the effects of the addition of videos to a website promoting environmental breast-cancer risk reduction practices: Are videos worth it? *Journal of Applied Communication Research*, *42*, 20–40.

Pratkanis, A., & Anderson, E. (2001). *Age of propaganda*. New York, NY: Henry Holt.

Pries, L. (2017). *La transnacionalización del mundo social: Espacios sociales más allá de las sociedades nacionales*. México: Colegio de México.

Reed, H. (1998). *Immigrant assimilation and health insurance coverage in the United States* (Master's thesis). Georgetown University.

Reed, H. E., & Yrizar Barbosa, G. (2017). Investigating the refugee health disadvantage among the U.S. immigrant population. *Journal of Immigrant & Refugee Studies*, *15*, 53–70.

Rice, R. A., & Robinson, J. A. (2013). Transdisciplinary approaches for twenty-first-century ocean sustainability communication. In R. E. Rice & C. K. Atkin (Eds.), *Public communication campaigns* (4th ed., pp. 231–244). Thousand Oaks, CA: Sage Publications.

Rice, R. E., & Atkin, C. K. (2013). *Public communication campaigns* (4th ed., pp. 53–68). Thousand Oaks, CA: Sage Publications.

Ries, A., & Trout, J. (1986). *Positioning: The battle for your mind*. New York, NY: Warner.

Robson, C. (2010). *Real world research*. London: Blackwell.

Rodriguez, C. (2017). Enforcement, integration, and the future of immigration federalism. *Journal of Migration and Human Security*, *5*, 509–540.

Rodríguez, M. A., Young, M. E., & Wallace, S. P. (2015, April). Creating conditions to support healthy people: State policies that affect the health of undocumented immigrants and their families. Los Angeles, CA: UC Global Health Institute, UCLA Blum Center for Poverty and Health in Latin America, and UCLA Center for Health Policy and Research.

Rogers, E. M. (2003). *Diffusion of innovations* (5th ed.). New York, NY: Free Press.

Romero Sanchez, G. (2017, July 3). Apoyó el gobierno capitalino a 20 mil deportados en seis meses. La Jornada. www.jornada.com.mx/2017/07/03/capital/029n1cap

Rubin, M. (2009). *From Puebla to East Harlem: Healthcare for a rapidly emerging community.* New York, NY: Academy of Medicine.

Sabogal, F., & Cordingley-Klein, J. (1999). Ethnic social marketing for elderly minorities: Challenges and opportunities. *Social Marketing Quarterly, 5,* 30–39.

Sack, K. (2009, December 31). For sick illegal immigrants, no relief back home. *New York Times.* www.nytimes.com/2010/01/01/health/policy/01grady.html

Salgado, N., Riosmena, F., González-Block, M. A., & Wong, R. (2012, October 15–17). Vulnerabilidad en salud durante el proceso de migración: Implicaciones para las políticas de salud en México y Estados Unidos. Presentation at the Fifth National Migration Week. México.

Sánchez-Siller, I. M., & Gabarrot-Arenas, M. (2014). ¿Exclusión en los dos lados? Un análisis de las políticas de salud para migrantes mexicanos en Estados Unidos desde una perspectiva binacional. *Revista Gerencia y Políticas de Salud, 13,* 147–167.

Sanders, H. (2014). Immigrants and the rights to health in New York City since the 1990s: A case of "urban citizenship." In M. Tanrisal & T. E. Tunc (Eds.), *The health of the American nation: An historical, cultural and literary survey* (pp. 106–116). Heidelberg: Universitätsverlag.

Schmid, C. L. (2017). The past is ever present: Transnationalism old and new—Italian and Mexican immigrants in the United States. *International Migration, 55,* 20–37.

Schmitter, B. (1985). Sending countries and the politics of emigration and destination. *International Migration Review, 19,* 469–484.

Schmitter Heisler, B. (1984). Sending states and immigrant minorities. The case of Italy. *Comparative Studies of Society and History, 26,* 325–334.

SRE [Secretaría de Relaciones Exteriores]. (2011a). Informe de México: Avances y desafíos en materia de derechos humanos. www.upr-info.org/followup/assessments/session17/mexico/Mexico-InformHR.pdf

SRE (2011b). Segundo informe periódico de México sobre el cumplimiento de la convención internacional sobre la protección de los derechos de todos los trabajadores migratorios y sus familias. http://sre.gob.mx/sre-docs/dh/docsdh/informes/4617txt.pdf

SRE (2015). Guía de procedimientos de protección consular. Dirección General de Protección a Mexicanos en el Exterior. www.gob.mx/cms/uploads/attachment/file/109345/Gu_a_de_Procedimientos_de_Protecci_n_Consular.pdf

Secretaría de Salud. (n.d.) Pamphlet or comic book about Seguro Popular distributed by Ventanillas de Salud [Health Windows] in Mexican consulates by the 2006–2012 federal government.

Secretaría de Salud & Seguro Popular. (2014, February). Informe de resultados del sistema de protección social en salud 2013. Gaceta de la Cámara de Diputados 62. http://gaceta.diputados.gob.mx/Gaceta/62/2014/feb/Inf_SS-20140205.pdf

Seelig, A., Jacobson, I., Smith, B., Hooper, T., Boyko, E., Gackstetter, G., ... Smith, T. (2010). Sleep patterns in military personnel before, during and after deployment to Iraq and Afghanistan. *Sleep, 33,* 1615–1622.

Sharma, J. (2006). Características de la diáspora india y su relación con el país de origen. In C. González Gutiérrez (Ed.), *Relaciones estado–diáspora: Aproximaciones desde cuatro continentes* (Vol. 1, pp. 65–97). Mexico: Miguel Ángel Porrúa, UAZ, SRE, IME, ANUIES.

Shibata, H. (2015). *A tale of two states: A historical institutional analysis on the shifting transnational connections of the Brazilian Nikkei* (Doctoral dissertation). CUNY Graduate Center.

Shifman, L. (2012). An anatomy of a YouTube meme. *New Media & Society, 14,* 187–203.

Shtarkshall, R. A., Baynesan, F., & Feldman, B. S. (2009). A socio-ecological analysis of Ethiopian immigrants' interactions with the Israeli healthcare system and its policy and service implications. *Ethnicity & Health, 14,* 459–478.

Siegel, M., & Donor, L. (1998). *Marketing public health: Strategies to promote social change.* Gaithersburg, MD: Aspen.

Singal, J. (2014, July 17). Awareness is overrated. *New York Magazine.* http://nymag.com/scienceofus/2014/07/awareness-is-overrated.html

Small, M. L. (2009). "How many cases do I need?" On science and the logic of case selection in field-based research. *Ethnography, 10,* 5–38.

Smith, B. (2002). Social marketing and its potential contribution to a modern synthesis of social change. *Social Marketing Quarterly, 8,* 46–48.

Smith, B. (2003). Beyond "health" as a benefit. *Social Marketing Quarterly, 9,* 22–28.

Smith, B. (2012). American politics and social marketing: A candid conversation with Philip Kotler and Bill Novelli. *Social Marketing Quarterly, 18,* 3–8.

Smith, R. C. (1995). *Counting migrant farmworkers: Causes of the undercount of farmworkers in the northeastern United States in the 1990 census and strategies to increase coverage for census 2000.* Final report to Center for Survey Methods Research. Washington, DC: Statistical Research Division, Bureau of the Census..

Smith, R. C. (1998). Transnational localities: Community, technology and the politics of membership within the context of Mexico and US migration. In M. P. Smith & L. E. Guarnizo (Eds.), *Transnationalism from below* (pp. 196–238). New Brunswick, NJ: Transaction.

Smith, R. C. (2003a). Migrant membership as an instituted process: Transnationalization, the state and the extra-territorial conduct of Mexican politics. *International Migration Review, 37,* 297–343.

Smith, R. C. (2003b). Diasporic membership in historical perspective: Comparative insights from the Mexican, Italian and Polish cases. *International Migration Review, 37,* 724–759.

Smith, R. C. (2006). *Mexican New York: Transnational worlds of new immigrants.* Berkeley, CA: University of California Press.

Smith, R. C. (2008). Contradictions of diasporic institutionalization in Mexican politics: The 2006 migrant vote and other forms of inclusion and control. *Ethnic and Racial Studies, 31,* 708–741.

Smith, R. C. (2013). Mexicans: Civic engagement, education, and progress achieved and inhibited. In N. Foner (Ed.), *One out of three: Immigrant New York in the twenty-first century* (pp. 246–266). New York, NY: Columbia University Press.

Smith, R. C. (2019). Hawthorne effects in ethnography: Epistemology, ethics, and scientific validity. Paper to be presented at the American Sociological Association Meetings, August 2019, New York.

Smith, R. C., & Seguro Popular Team. (2012). *Estudio del nivel de información sobre el Seguro Popular con que cuenta la población migrante mexicana de la Ciudad de Nueva York, EE.UU.* Final report to the Centro de Investigación y Docencia Económica, Mexico City and Seguro Popular. Baruch College, School of Public Affairs.

Smith, R. C., Waisanen, D., Yrizar Barbosa, G., Lucero, A., & Castro, M. (2012). *Estudio para analizar una estrategia de difusión sobre el Seguro Popular dirigida a migrantes mexicanos en Nueva York.* Final report to the Centro de Investigación y Docenia Económica, Mexico City and Seguro Popular. Baruch College, School of Public Affairs.

Snow, D., & Benford, R. (1992). Master frames and cycles of protest. In A. D. Morris & C. McClurg Mueller (Eds.), *Frontiers of social movement theory* (pp. 133–155). New Haven, CT: Yale University Press.

Snyder, L. B., & LaCroix, J. M. (2013). How effective are mediated health campaigns? A synthesis of meta-analyses. In R. E. Rice & C. K. Atkin (Eds.), *Public communication campaigns* (4th ed., pp. 113–132). Thousand Oaks, CA: Sage Publications.

Solé, C. (1995). Portugal and Spain: From exporters to importers of labour. In R. Cohen (Ed.), *The Cambridge survey of world migration* (pp. 316–320). Cambridge: Cambridge University Press.

Somers, M. (1994). The narrative constitution of identity. *Theory and Society, 23,* 605–649.

Sosa-Rubí, S., Galárraga, O., & López-Ridaura, R. (2009). Diabetes treatment and control: The effect of the public health insurance for the poor in Mexico. *Bulletin of the World Health Organization, 87,* 512–519.

Spano, R. (2006). Observer behavior as a potential source of reactivity: Describing and quantifying observer effects in a large-scale observational study of police. *Sociological Methods & Research, 34,* 521–553.

Sugarman, S., Backman, D., Foerster, S. B., Ghirardelli, A., Linares, A., & Fong, A. (2011). Using an opinion poll to build an obesity-prevention social marketing campaign for low-income Asian and Hispanic immigrants. *Journal of Nutrition Education and Behavior, 43,* S53–S66.

Suman 13 mil repatriados de EU afiliados al Seguro Popular. (2017, May 16). Radio Formula. www.radioformula.com.mx/noticias/20170516/suman-13-mil-repatriados-de-eu-afiliados-al-seguro-popular/

Thaler, R. H., & Sunstein, C. R. (2008). *Nudge*. New Haven, CT: Yale University Press.

Ubel, P. (2010). Beyond costs and benefits: Understanding how patients make health-care decisions. *Oncologist, 15*, 5–10.

Uribe, M., Rodríguez, K., & Agudelo, M. (2013). *Determinantes sociales y acceso a los servicios de salud sexual y reproductiva en el Seguro Popular: Estudio de caso en el municipio de León*. Buenos Aires, Argentina: CLACSO Latin American Council of Social Sciences..

U.S.–Mexico Border Health Commission. (n.d.). U.S. Department of Health and Human Services. www.hhs.gov/about/agencies/oga/about-oga/what-we-do/international-relations-division/americas/border-health-commission/index.html

Valdes de Montano, L. M., & Smith, R. C. (1994). Mexicans in New York: Final report to the Tinker Foundation. New York.

Vargas Bustamante, A., Laugesen, M., Caban, M., & Rosenau, P. (2012). United States–Mexico cross-border health insurance initiatives: Salud Migrante and Medicare in Mexico. *Revista Panamericana de Salud Pública, 31*(1), 74–80.

Varsanyi, M. (Ed.). (2010). *Taking local control: Immigration policy activism in U.S. cities and states*. Stanford, CA: Stanford University Press.

Vázquez, M. L., Terraza-Núñez, R., Vargas, I., Rodríguez, D., & Lizana, T. (2011). Health policies for migrant populations in three European countries: England, Italy and Spain. *Health Policy, 101*, 70–78.

Waisanen, D. (2012). Bordering populism in immigration activism: Outlaw-civic discourse in a (counter)public. *Communication Monographs, 79*, 232–255.

Waisanen, D. J. (2009). Facebook, diasporic-virtual publics, and networked argumentation. In D. Gouran (Ed.), *The functions of argument and social context* (pp. 550–556). Washington, DC: National Communication Association.

Waisanen, D. J. (2011). Argument ecologies in social media: Populist reason in Facebook immigration pages. In R. Rowland (Ed.), *Reasoned argument and social change* (pp. 715–722). Washington, DC: National Communication Association.

Waisanen, D. J. (2019). Arguments for everybody: Social media, context collapse, and the universal audience. In R. Lake (Ed.), *Recovering argument* (pp. 264–269). New York, NY: Routledge.

Waisanen, D. J., Hahn, A., & Gander, E. (2019). Text, talk, argue: How to improve text-driven political conversations. In C. Winkler (Ed.), *Networking argument*. New York, NY: Routledge.

Waisbord, S. (2015). Three challenges for communication and global social change. *Communication Theory, 25*, 144–165.

Waldinger, R. (2015). *The cross-border connection: Immigrants, emigrants, and their homelands*. Cambridge, MA: Harvard University Press.

Weinreich, N. K. (2010). *Hands-on social marketing: A step-by-step guide to designing change for good*. Thousand Oaks, CA: Sage Publications.

Weissman, D., Hagan, J., Martinez-Schuldt, R., & Peavey, A. (2018). The politics of immigrant rights: Between political geography and transnational interventions. *Michigan State Law Review*, 117–187.

Wenburg, J. R., & Wilmot, W. W. (1973). *The personal communication process.* New York, NY: Wiley.

Wilkinson, S. (1998). Focus groups in health research: Exploring meanings of health and illness. *Journal of Health Psychology*, *3*, 329–348.

Williams, J. D., & Kumanyika, S. K. (2003). Is social marketing an effective tool to reduce health disparities? *Social Marketing Quarterly*, *8*, 14–31.

Wilson, F., Stimpson, J. P., & Pagan, J. A. (2014). Disparities in health outcomes of return migrants in Mexico. *International Journal of Population*, 1–9.

Winship, C., & Morgan, S. L. (1999). The estimation of causal effects from observational data. *Annual Review of Sociology*, *25*, 659–706.

Witte, K. (1992). Putting the fear back into fear appeals: The extended parallel process model. *Communication Monographs*, *59*, 329–349.

Yrizar Barbosa, G. (2008). *De la repatriación de cadáveres al voto extraterritorial: Política de emigración y gobiernos estatales en el Centro Occidente de México* (Master's thesis). Colegio de la Frontera Norte.

Yrizar Barbosa, G. (2009). Políticas migratorias e instituciones hacia los marroquíes en el extranjero: ¿Amenaza política o panacea transfronteriza? *Frontera Norte*, *21*, 53–77.

Yrizar Barbosa, G. (2018). Birds of passage no longer? The Mexican population of New York City, 2000–2015. Latino Data Report #73. Center for Latin American, Caribbean and Latino Studies, CUNY.

Yrizar Barbosa, G., & Alarcón, R. (2010). Emigration policy and state governments in Mexico. *Migraciones Internacionales*, *5*, 165–198.

Yrizar Barbosa, G., Smith, R. C., & Reed, H. E. (2016, March 31). Assessing geographic dispersion and limited inclusion in New York City: DACA and the MIDA. Presented at the Population Association of America, annual meeting, session P5. Washington, DC.

Zillman, D. (2006). Exemplification effects in the promotion of safety and health. *Journal of Communication*, *56*, 221–237.

Zolberg, A. (2006). *A nation by design: Immigration policy in the fashioning of America*. Cambridge, MA: Harvard University Press.

Zuñiga, V. (2015). Niños y adolescentes separados de sus familias por la migración internacional: El caso de cuatro estados de México. *Estudios Sociológicos*, *33*, 145–168.

Zuñiga, V., & Hamann, E. T. (2008). Escuelas nacionales, alumnos transnacionales: La migración México/Estados Unidos como fenómeno escolar. *Estudios Sociológicos*, *26*(76), 65–85.

Index

Note: Figures and photos are indicated by **bold** page numbers; tables are indicated by *italicized* page numbers.

For Product Safety Concerns and Information please contact our EU
representative GPSR@taylorandfrancis.com
Taylor & Francis Verlag GmbH, Kaufingerstraße 24, 80331 München, Germany